FEATHERS
FROM
MY *N*EST

FEATHERS FROM MY NEST

A MOTHER'S REFLECTIONS

BETH MOORE

BROADMAN
&HOLMAN
PUBLISHERS

NASHVILLE, TENNESSEE

0-8054-2464-4

Published by Broadman & Holman Publishers, Nashville, Tennessee

Dewey Decimal Classification: 248.8

Subject Heading: MOTHERS AND CHILDREN / HOME—CHRISTIAN LIFE

Library of Congress Card Catalog Number: 00-066709

Unless otherwise stated all Scripture citation is from the New International Version, copyright © 1973, 1978, 1984 by International Bible Society. Other versions cited include the King James Version.

Library of Congress Cataloging-in-Publication Data

Moore, Beth, 1957–

  Feathers from my nest : a mother's reflections / Beth Moore.

    p. cm.

  ISBN 0-8054-2464-4

    1. Mothers—Religious life.   2. Christian life—Baptist authors.   3. Moore, Beth, 1957– 4. Home—Religious aspects—Christianity. I. Title.

  BV4529.18 .M66   2001

  248.8'431—dc21

                                       00-066709

1 2 3 4 5 6 7 8 9 10 11 12 13 14 15   05 04 03 02 01

To all the sparrows that stopped by my nest

ACKNOWLEDGMENTS

I wish I had words to properly express my gratitude to God for His amazing redemption and unreasonable mercy in my life. The opportunity to minister through these pages is nothing less than a grace gift of God that I never want to take for granted. He has forgiven me for so much. How I desire to love much in return. Second only to my gratitude to God, I am so thankful for the lavish love, joy, and support I constantly receive from my beloved husband and daughters. Keith, Amanda, and Melissa, God as surely chose you as He chose me. Thank you for not only allowing me to speak, teach, and write, but for being a critical part of everything God has called me to do. This book wouldn't even exist without you. Thank you for sharing my conviction that transparency and vulnerability are worth the help and encouragement they lend to others. All three of you are such good sports. What other family would have let me tell so much on them? You are the best and I am nuts over you.

I am also deeply grateful for the love and support I receive on a daily basis from my staff at Living Proof Ministries. Thank you Kim, Susan, Sabrina, Diane, Kimberly, Nancy, Julie, and Mary Helen for doing your jobs so thoroughly that I am free to do mine. Thanks so much for letting me bounce some of these excerpts off of you. And for laughing and crying with me. You are my ministry family and I thank God continually for all of you. Steve Seelig, I also want to thank you, brother. You were the one God first used to ever even suggest the idea of publishing a book to me. I haven't written a single trade book without your input. Have we had a wild ride, or what? You remain a constant source of encouragement to me.

Lastly, I wish to thank the team at Broadman & Holman for being so willing to partner in creative works like this one with me. You guys are so great. Thanks for making this possible.

*Now unto Him that is able to do exceeding
abundantly above all that we ask or think . . . be
glory in the church by Christ Jesus throughout all
ages, world without end. Amen.*
EPHESIANS 3:20–21 KJV

CONTENTS

FEATHERS FROM MY NEST

"Make haste, my dear Mrs. Sparrow. The wind is picking up. Let's be on our way!"

"Another moment! I'm almost finished. Any sign of them?"

"No, dear love. Not in the half a breeze since you last inquired."

"I just hate to leave too soon. What if . . . ?"

"What if what, my love? What if they fly back home after we have raised them to climb the wind?"

"But they may have forgotten. . . ."

"Forgotten what, my love? They took everything they needed. Had they taken any more, their wings could not have carried the burden."

"But the little one, Mr. Sparrow. She was so young. Her flight seemed a little unsure. I saw her look back, I did!"

"Yes, dear one, because she continued to hear you sing her song. She is young, yes. But she is strong just like her sister. You'll see. Fine sparrows they are, dear Mrs. Let them fly."

"As if I could have stopped them."

"Oh, dear Mrs. Sparrow, you know better. You could have clipped their tail feathers with your pecking. You could have refused to let them test their wings on the early gentle breezes. You could have done much to stop them, but you didn't. Their flight was perfectly timed, my Mrs., but I fear we will miss *ours* if we do not get on our way. What ever are you doing now?"

"Just another moment! Let me tidy up. I'm almost finished."

"Dear Mrs., the nest was already tidy."

"Yes! Far too tidy for a mother's taste. A nest is built for chicks . . . and plenty of them!"

"Dear, dear one, not more tears! Will you cry until you have clouded your vision? Come! Let this delightful autumn breeze dry your eyes. We still have heights to climb. Gaze up, dear Mrs., to your maker. Will He not see them if they fall? Is He not compassionate to all He has made? He is above you and I am right beside you. You'll be fine. Now, come along, my love."

"Very well, then. I suppose I'm ready."

Mrs. Sparrow joined him on the branch, attempting to stay somewhat obscured behind a golden leaf.

"Dear Mrs., what ever have you done? Your wings are bulging. You look more like a plump robin in spring than my slender sparrow!" Mr. Sparrow chirped with warm affection. "What are you hiding under there?"

"Never you mind. Let's be on our way!"

"Mrs. Sparrow, we've flown together far too many seasons for secrets. Out with it! What have you done?"

"Well, if you must know, I've gathered feathers from my

nest. They left a few behind and I'm taking them ahead. I am and that settles it."

Mr. Sparrow chose a wise pause.

"Very well then, Madame."

"Where are you going, Mr. Sparrow?"

"Now it is your turn to wait, dear Mrs. I'll be back in two shakes of a tail feather." With one thrust of his strong wings, Mr. Sparrow was back at the nest they had shared for so long. He perched on its side for a time by himself, memories swirling like the autumn wind.

"Hurry, Mr. Sparrow! It's time! I can feel the wind rising."

"Ah, now *you're* in a rush! Give me a moment as well." He gazed at the nest, simple but sturdy. They hadn't known it was sturdy until it stood the test of time. Harsh weather. Wind and rain. But the sunlight never failed to return, bringing healing to their wings. His knowing eyes returned to a mark on the branch left by a young sparrow that had been dropped off by the wind. They tried to make him theirs, but he was a child of the wind. His flight from the nest came early and suddenly. He wondered again where the young sparrow's wings would take him and prayed for the wind to be kind.

"Dear Mister, what are you doing?"

Mr. Sparrow brushed his eyes with the tip of his wing before the Mrs. could catch him. He then spied exactly what he needed—a string intertwined in the bowl-shaped twigs. He reached it with his beak, pulling it forth with a tug and a snap. He returned to his Mrs. who did not appear to have lightened her load a single feather.

"Up with your wings, Mrs. Sparrow."

"Whatever for?"

"If you insist on taking those feathers, at least allow me to tie them around you so that you are still free to soar." She slowly lifted her wings, feeling a little silly, but safe with her mister. He bound them as close as he could to her heart then tied the string with a double-knotted bow on her back. His tender care told Mrs. Sparrow that he was quite unopposed to the keepsakes. A fresh wind blew, and two auburn leaves detached from the branch and danced their way to the ground. "That's our ride, Mrs. Sparrow. Let's be on our way."

They lifted up effortlessly into the sky and headed toward a masterfully painted horizon. Mr. Sparrow glanced back one last time. "A fine nest it was." Mrs. Sparrow was finally content to look ahead, her tears drying in the autumn breeze. There would be more tears. But there would also be more breezes to dry them. She looked to her right content-edly, thankful for her partner in this terrestrial flight. She then tilted her wings upward to gaze toward her Maker, assured of her flight's destination. No need to look back. After all, she left nothing behind. For she had gathered feathers from her nest.

"Are not two sparrows sold for a penny?

Yet not one of them will fall to the ground apart

from the will of your Father. . . .

So don't be afraid . . ."

MATTHEW 10:29, 31

These are feathers from my nest.

Amanda and I on her first day of
kindergarten letting the bus driver
know to "Stop here!"

The Moores and each of our best
friends at Christmas of 1999.

CHAPTER I

Wood, Brick, and Mortar

"Do you have a normal home just like anybody else?" The question caught me off guard. My first thought was of how few "anybody else's" I know who have the illusive "normal home." Does a normal *house* count? Now, *that* I've got. Just a regular, family-raising enclosure with no few pets in the yard. A little wood, a little brick, a little mortar, and a lot of fur. Same house we've had for seventeen years and most of the same pets. Yes, I'd say the Moores qualify for a normal *house,* but it's the *home* part that might stick an *ab* onto the front of that aggravating *N* word. Let's be realistic. If the experts on Christian family dynamics are looking for "normal," they might want to skip the Moore home.

Normal? Not particularly. Functional? Uh, what does that mean? It sounds more like an appliance to me. My dishwasher was functional, but it still broke after seven measly years. My children, who are certainly "fun," if not the poster children for "functional," are still kicking . . . and sometimes even screaming. No, I'm not sure we're particularly normal or perfectly functional, but happy? Ah, yes. At least we were this morning. We've got a lot of daylight yet for all that to change. Anyway, if we're not happy, please don't tell us. We're doing just fine thinking that we are.

Maybe we have a skewed idea of what happy *is,* but something is working for us. All four of us possess salvation in Christ alone and will spend eternity together in heaven. We practice mutual respect. I might add that practice has yet to make perfect. We laugh our heads off. And gladly at the other person's expense. We agree on some things. Disagree on plenty of others. And, right or wrong, feel some measure of freedom to express it. Did I mention *passionately?* On top of all that, none of us spent last weekend in jail, but even if one of us had, I suppose we would make it through that too.

Maybe that's the key phrase. *Making it.* I don't know how you feel about those two words, but I happen to think they're huge. Since the first day my children went to Mother's Day Out, I dreaded the proverbial empty nest like a terminal disease. I literally collapsed on the mailbox when the school bus had the gall to kidnap my kindergartners. Honestly, I worried about myself. I thought, *If you're acting this way now, what in the world are you going to do when they go to college?* Sure enough, that day came way too soon, but I did not sink into despair. Oh, I cried all right. But that first quiet morning when I had no children to awaken for school, I felt some things I didn't expect. Like gratitude. Overwhelming gratitude. I sat before God with tears streaming down my cheeks and three words fell unexpectedly from my lips over and over:

We made it. And not just by the skin of our teeth. I might as well confess that I'm not much of a martyr. Even when I sacrifice something for Christ, I go running to the throne as fast as I can to gain all the more of Him. Somehow, I have to hope there's more to life than simply surviving misery and just barely making it through life.

I realized that first morning in my empty nest that we didn't just survive. We made it. Our children loaded up their cars for college and pulled out of a driveway made of concrete solidified by time. Our girls left a home made of more than wood, brick, and mortar. Oddly, we never even realized how solid it was until years of harsh weather were unable to destroy it. No few times life had come to huff and puff and blow our house down. Keith and I took turns holding up walls depending upon who had the strength that season. At times I feared we were the *four* little pigs (some bigger than others) in a house made of straw, but time proved otherwise. You can be sure that the reason we made it wasn't because we held up the walls but because, to do so, we had to stand squarely upon the foundation beneath our feet. A certain Rock.

The first morning I awakened to a house with no children, my home was quiet, but to my surprise it wasn't empty. Suddenly it felt full. Full of memories. Full of anticipation. Full of a love that can somehow go with them to college and beyond yet stay back home with us. A love that has a name. *Jesus.* I knew we had made it because of Him. My heart poured forth like a busted pipe saturating every room and soaking the carpet with gratitude. I glanced at an old picture on the wall that Keith and I had received as a wedding gift. It was hanging on the dark paneling of our first little dwelling when we came home from our honeymoon. The picture has moved from place to place with us and only grows more conspicuous. While all the surrounding furnishings change, the orange and brown paint on this picture reflects the same 1970s style that marked the groomsmen's tuxes at our wedding. Let's see if I can say this nicely: It's just plain ugly. The words on the picture, however, are priceless—*timeless.* "Except the LORD build the house, they labour in vain that build it" (Ps. 127:1 KJV).

That picture has hung on the wall through every fight, every struggle, and every battle for control we've ever experienced. Sometimes it hung lopsided because someone slammed a door, but it always hung in there. It was nailed to the wall when everything else was shaking. I find it so peculiar—and so *like God*—that our remedy was right there all along, speaking truth over us and calling out to us in a quiet but powerful inflection. Its words were the still, small voice in the midst of the rolling thunder. *Except the Lord build the house, they labour in vain that build it.* Perhaps you may be as relieved as I am that the Hebrew word for *build* in this verse also means "repair." At times ours was a home in desperate need of repair because ours were *hearts* in desperate need of repair. The process has been painful, but I wouldn't trade it for anything. God could have performed an instant miracle of healing upon our hearts and our home, but I hate to think what we would have missed. We've been right there with Him, holding the shingles in place while God nailed them down. Holding the sloshing paint bucket while God slapped a new coat on the walls. We haven't missed a thing. Neither has the picture. It has hung there long enough to see not only the struggles but to witness the change, hear the laughter, and feel the warmth of the sunshine pouring through the opened windows. The chill is gone.

That we've made it several decades doesn't guarantee we'll make it several more, but we've still got all the tools for rebuilding out in the toolshed. And we certainly know whom to contract for the labor. After all, He's a carpenter by trade. We know how to make it if we're willing: start handing Him the pieces. If we don't, it will be a lack of obedience, not a lack of knowledge. To us, making it means that we each cast our votes in favor of family . . . even when we vote for different things in life. We love and *confess our love* to one another almost daily. We don't just let love and mutual concern develop naturally. I've learned that the things that develop "naturally" are usually the things of the human nature, not the Holy Spirit's. We've worked hard at "family." We've had to. We had so many strikes against us that the umpire was practically yelling "Out!" before we stepped up to bat.

One of my deepest desires in putting these thoughts on paper is to encourage you in your own family journey. Beloved, with the intervention of God and a lot of cooperation, unstable families can become stable. Emotionally dangerous homes can become safe houses of gentler candor. Homes shattered by loss can echo once again with laughter. Peace can replace chaos . . . but you must promise not to confuse peace with quiet. The goal is not building a monastery. Remember, God's peace is like a *river,* not a pond. In other words, a sense of health and well-being, both of which are expressions of the Hebrew *shalom,* can permeate our homes even when we're in white-water rapids.

God can change the entire dynamics of a household. He really can make an unhealthy family *healthy*. I know because His Word says it's true. I know because He's done it for us. Centuries of generational bondage can be broken and descendants blessed because of one generation's willingness to work hard with God to change. Those who welcome the healing work of God can "rebuild the ancient ruins and restore the places long devastated" (Isa. 61:4). Keith and I brought enough accumulated baggage into our house to crack the foundation . . . except that inch by inch the foundation became Christ. And He's simply uncrackable. You don't have the one family God can't transform. And, no, not every person in the household has to be willing and cooperative for change to begin. I will ask you this: Are you?

Remodeling a home often begins with just one who is willing to pray, believe God, persevere, and be personally remodeled. Don't start trying to rebuild your whole family. Life's far too short to "labor in vain." Just allow God to rebuild *you*. Thankfully, health can be as contagious as sickness. Slowly you will begin to see the contagious effect of God's healing work. Perhaps you're thinking, *My marriage has already ended in divorce. It's too late for my family to make it.*

Beloved, do you still have family? Then it's not too late to start developing into a strong one. Not all members of each household have to be present for the remaining members to *make it*. I have a missing person too. A boy we raised for seven years. The son of my heart. Our household could have toppled to the ground over the change—all the complicated emotions and regrets involved. But what a tragedy it would be to sacrifice what *remains* on the altar of what is *missing*. Search your house for what is present—even if it's the solitary person in the mirror. Single, married, divorced, widowed, orphaned—all of us are invited to relocate from the shifting sand and rebuild upon the Rock. No better time than before the next flood. In His account of the wise and foolish builders in Luke 6, Christ didn't imply the possibility of a flood but the *inevitability*. Rains *will* come, the waters *will* rise, and life's currents *will* pound furiously against our homes. Count on it. But there's one thing you can count on more than an inevitable flood. The Rock. "Trust in the LORD forever, for the LORD, the LORD, is the Rock eternal" (Isa. 26:4). "No, there is no other Rock; I know not one" (Isa. 44:8b).

Melissa and her Big Wheel.

Amanda and her bike.

Anywhere big wheels and bikes could not
take them, Mom was sure to go.

CHAPTER 2

127,000 MILES

One of the things my children left behind when they flew the coop was a billion miles on my '91 Moore-mobile. OK. So it was only 127,000. But I felt every mile of it. In fact, I'm *still* feeling it since I'm *still* driving it. Present active participle verb tense: *130,000 miles and counting.* Keith suggested that I might need to wait until someone graduates from college to shop for a replacement. Will *any* someone do? Or does it have to be one of ours? And what if that "someone" ends up cramming four years into six, I ask you?

But don't think the man doesn't practice what he preaches. Keith didn't give up his last truck until it had a good, round 200,000 miles on it. At 150,000 miles, I told him it was time for a new one. He said that it was just getting "broken in." What man calls "broken in," woman calls "broken down." Between Keith and me we have some serious frequent driver miles, but the difference is that most of Keith's miles accrued between here and the deer lease. Mine are the consequence of that modern-day road hazard called *carpool*—a sinister plot of the male population to drive the women of America out of the workforce and into a home for unfed mothers.

It's time the public knew. Lives are at stake. It's not that the mother *can't* drive. It's that no one in the car will let her. A carpool driver rarely faces the front. You may never see her face, but her body can be recognized in double-jointed contortions over the seat, index finger shaking violently. At first glance a passerby might ask, "Was that a woman bent over the seat wearing her pajamas?" Yes, but she'll tell you they're her workout clothes. A cover-up. And that's only the beginning.

Oh, the things that run through her mind between the drop-off zone and Kroger. "What if the kids tell their mothers about the ticket I got for speeding through the school zone?" "What if Chelsea tells her mother that I accidentally called her a brat? What rhymes with *brat?*" No one knows her secret pain. She eventually develops a tic, but that's not the worst of it. She begins dressing to match her minivan. She used to be normal. It's not her fault. But it *is* her responsibility. *Carpool.* That perilous rite of passage in modern motherhood that hasn't reached its full potential until you would gladly drive your car into the nearest pool. *While in it.*

Trust me. I put in my time. Between three children, not only did I often work double time on overlapping shifts; I drove to three different schools. I am pretty certain I've done more road time than Charles Kuralt. You too? As much as I hate to, I bet I can one-up you. One of my children's schools was seventeen miles from home—smack in the middle of Houston's rush hour traffic. Right here is where I win the prize: *It was my "boy" carpool.* Now for my really disturbing confession: *I loved it.*

Don't get me wrong. It was a pain! All the rushing around in the morning because someone else's mother is depending on you. Rushing only to wait in the driveway for ten solid minutes on sweet little so-and-so. All the help they are when they learn to read the speed limit sign and match it with your speedometer. "Mrs. Moore, are you speeding?" "Of course not, darling." Then there's all the noise. All the fighting. Or worse yet, all the getting along, which usually entails something obnoxious like wrestling, sticking stuff in their noses, or playing a friendly game of seeing how long the other one can go without yelling when he's punched. (Yes, *really.*) Nobody likes the same music or the same volume. "Turn it up, Mrs. Moore. I can't even hear it." "Turn it down, Mrs. Moore. It's hurting my ears."

Only God and the attendance office know how many times I had to sign them in late—marching into the school like the Pied Piper, with a line of munchkins behind me. And that was only the morning shift. Nothing compares with the humiliation of everyone staring as you burn rubber turning into the pickup lane in the afternoon. I never had to honk for my carload. They just listened for my tires to squeal. All the way there, I'd be thinking, *It can't possibly be three o'clock already. I just dropped them off! For heaven's sake, what are we paying these teachers?* (Not nearly enough.) I have no idea if I left a lasting impression on the children, but I certainly left one on the pavement in front of the Baptist Academy. Look, I had a lot on my mind! Like trying to keep up with whose turn it was to sit in the front. Let's face it. That's *real* stress. The folks at the New York Stock Exchange think they have stress? They should take a turn in the carpool, shouldn't they, girls?

But if we could just see the forest for the trees. Carpool analogy? If we would just see the children for the challenge . . . how blessed we would be! My mother believed to her dying day that it was a sad woman indeed that didn't have a young child somewhere in her life. She also felt there was no excuse for *not* having one. If you didn't have one handy, you could *get* one—in Sunday school, in a church nursery, a pint-size human who lives down the street—all the while, relieving a young mom and adding something worth more than a hill of beans to your life. She'd tell you that you could find a child almost anywhere you find a lot of *life*. But find one indeed. Because to her, you would be a miserable soul if you lost touch with children. I am deeply indebted to my mother for teaching me that one way to be rich was to be rich in children. And, thank goodness, they don't all have to be your own. In that case, carpool made me a veritable magnate.

Monday was one of my carpool days. Then again, between all three children, so were Tuesday, Wednesday, and Thursday—and often Friday mornings if I wasn't heading to the airport. Mondays were my favorite. For starters, "Monday" usually meant I drove on the first day of school. I got to see them in their brand-new frocks. They were cuter than a litter of puppies. It was the only time all year that the little boys still had their shirts tucked in when they got into the car. I think they got the "double tuck" on the first day. (That means tucked into the underwear too.) Their hair was always slicked back and still wet, giving them that "miniature man" look. I wasn't fooled, though. It's so hard to find a manly looking lunch box. And they would have died if they'd known their mother's good-bye kiss was still lingering in "Passion Fruit Pink" right on their forehead. Thankfully, the thought of looking into a mirror hadn't yet entered their mind. Soon they would have to break Mother's heart anyway. There would be new first-grade teachers fresh out of college to fall in love with.

And the little girls? Now, *they* put the *A* in accessories. Each had her own theme going. Barrettes matched the lunch box that matched the backpack that matched the socks. The dress, selected weeks earlier, was the main attraction around which the whole look revolved. Their shoes were the one place the ensemble could go awry. No matter how prissy the outfit was, the girls preferred their new athletic shoes to their new dress shoes . . . much to Mother's dismay. The early shoe drama is only the beginning of the mother-daughter closet conflict.

Little boys and little girls. As different as night and day. Except that neither were very anxious to leave their mothers on the first day of school. As hard as it was to look past their new frocks, I also could detect the apprehension on their faces and the death grip on their mommies' necks. That's when my maternal hormones would produce a double portion. My mom taught me how to temporarily become someone else's: a momentary surrogate to offer a little one a helping hand in a hard transition. "Get in this car and show me those new school supplies! Would you look at that? I have never seen a finer backpack. Are you sure I'm supposed to be taking you to the elementary school? You look like you should be going to high school. Do you think Mrs. Moore could borrow that outfit? Could you drive while I look at all your new pencils?"

Magic moments. Carpool offers priceless opportunities for those. Seizing them just means we have to adopt a new goal. If you want to learn to enjoy a carload of kids, your goal must become something more than simply getting them to their destination *alive,* which is arguably no small accomplishment. Consider making the goal *engagement.* Engage in their lives, in their interests. Talk to them. And *listen.* Oh, what they teach us—not only about life in general but often about life at their particular address. Brace yourself while I make this next statement: You and I don't have a single family secret that hasn't been exposed in carpool. I can't count the times I've dropped off my carload and immediately dialed the phone to have a hearty laugh with a mom about what I just learned from her child. I never fail to like the children's version of the story better.

One of my favorite parts of carpool was the counsel the children offered one another. One of the little guys in my carpool was talking about how much he disliked the person he had to sit by in class. "Not only do I have to sit by a girl; she's ugly!" The other little boy, the much older age of nine, paused thoughtfully then said, "My dad says you'd better be careful about being mean to an ugly girl. She may grow up to be good-looking, and then you won't be able to get her for a date." He has one of the most beautiful moms you can imagine, so I just had to bait him. "Is that what happened to your daddy, Jonathan?" He said, "Nope. He must have been nice to Mom 'cause she ended up marrying him." Trust me. That woman has never had an ugly day in her life. I howled with laughter.

If you think you can learn from a carpool of elementary schoolers, you haven't lived until you've driven a carload of freshman girls, not old enough to drive but way too cool to ride the bus. You have to be sharp, though. They don't talk in real English, and they are forever telling each other what they already know: "Um, you know . . . you know . . . um, you know . . ." But if you listen carefully, those *"dot-dot-dots"* between the *"you knows"* can supply you more information than the *National Enquirer.* I knew who liked whom, who didn't like whom, and who went with whom, whether they liked them or not. I knew what was cool and what was not. I knew who could teach and who could not. Many times after they piled out of the car, I would watch them walk down the hall, talking a hundred miles an hour with their ponytails bouncing. Sometimes the tears would just stream down my cheeks. I had watched these little girls grow up since kindergarten. And what a fine job of growing up they were doing. They were indescribably precious.

I have no idea how many times one would stick her head back in the car and say, "Mrs. Moore, would you pray for me today? I have a *huge* test." Or, "Mrs. Moore, I don't feel very good. Please pray for me." In the midst of all the incessant chatter, something supernatural had happened. They caught on to the God of carpool. Somewhere between the backpacks, the purses, the hairbrushes, and the hormones, God made Himself room. What amazes me most is that usually He made Himself known through subtleties and snippets. Never through preaching but just plain everyday living. Through upbeat Christian contemporary music that many of the kids had never heard but were soon requesting and joining with singing. Through gentle diversions away from gossip. Through lots of joy, laughter, and encouragement. Through remarks about how majestically He had painted the sky that morning. Through promises to pray for them that day. Through naturally working His way into almost every conversation. God rode in our carpool, and to the praise of His faithful name, not one of them missed Him. Without exception every single one of those girls came to me around their high school graduation and told me how much their time in that overcrowded car meant to them. I cannot reflect upon their expressions without the tears stinging in my eyes. What a God of grace to allow me the privilege of driving for Him on a few of His road trips.

Those teenage girls were oblivious to my speaking schedule and had no idea I had ever written a book until they were practically out of high school. I don't think they would have cared anyway. I was simply Mrs. Moore, Amanda and Melissa's mom. I still hear from every one of them from time to time and have had the privilege of prayerfully supporting several through some difficult challenges in college. They are so dear to me. How thankful I am to have had daughters that never asked me to leave God at home when we drove carpool. He would have gone anyway—but what a pity it would have been for Him to ride silently. Instead, He found voice in all sorts of *low-key/high-glee* ways . . . and when all was said and done, those young girls were so glad He had come along. In Deuteronomy 6:7, God instructs us to talk about His precepts to our children "when you walk along the road." These days, we don't do a lot of walking. But we do *a lot* of driving. What prime opportunities to *engage* in a young life in Jesus' name. To me, that doesn't include beating them over the head with my Bible. Carpool is best driven with two hands on the wheel, a heart full of love, a soul full of joy, and a head full of discernment.

As much as I loved carpool, I certainly was thankful that other moms drove too. So were the kids, no doubt. Each one of those moms had something priceless to offer. One afternoon, I was watching the clock, wondering when that day's afternoon carpool would arrive with my boy. The time was getting to be uncharacteristically late. The phone rang and one of the other moms said, "Where in the world do you think they are?" I responded that I had no idea but I was getting worried. Then I asked, "Whose turn was it to drive? I don't have my list in front of me." She began digging through her kitchen drawer in search of her list. All of a sudden she screamed, "IT WAS *ME!*" *Click.* I laughed and laughed . . . and was so glad it wasn't *me.* It was time someone else left a tire mark on the pickup lane at the Baptist Academy.

Carpool. You gotta love it.

"Don't you just hate when life's supposed to be fun and it's not? Well, at least we have each other."

CHAPTER 3

THE CRUMPLED KLEENEX

The only thing as hard as watching your firstborn fly out of the nest is bracing yourself while your baby does the same. The first fall semester Amanda, our oldest daughter, was away, I woke up a half-dozen times or so in the middle of the night and felt like a change of scenery might help me sleep. Instead of moving to the guest room, I finished out the night in Amanda's bed. After all, the mattress was far more comfortable in her room. Well worn. It wasn't until later that a friend told me, "Don't you know that one of the most common things moms do after a child leaves is spend a handful of nights in his or her room? There's nothing new about that!" I was caught by total surprise. My heart's secret remedy was to get as close to her as I could by being surrounded by her things. Truth is always liberating even when it's a little embarrassing. Somehow once I recognized what kept driving me to move to her bed, I was free to stay in my own.

One of the last mornings I awakened in her room, I spotted a crumpled Kleenex under the edge of the bed as I was making it up. I had no idea how long it had been there, but I knew instinctively what it meant. She had been crying. Had the Kleenex been used for a cold, she would have left it crumpled on the bedside table. I know my child just like you know yours. If she stuck it under the bed, she had used it for her tears and didn't want anyone to know it. My heart ached. As I sat and stared at the evidence, I wondered what had caused those particular tears. A breakup with a boyfriend? Fears about going away to college? Had someone hurt her feelings? (And may I have a name and address, please?) Had *I* hurt her feelings? (God has my address.) Or was it something secret? Something I knew nothing about? Something she had suffered privately? I held the Kleenex in my hand and wondered what had broken her tender heart.

That's the hardest part of parenting. The heartache comes in double portions: knowing they hurt and hurting with them. Our first child was a big surprise, born nine and a half months after marriage to a mother who had been diagnosed with female problems that would require surgery to enable conception. *Yeah, right.* And was I ever glad they were wrong. As it turned out, *I did* end up requiring major surgery to be a mother. *Heart surgery.* Without anesthesia, I might add. God used my first child to slice away the thick layers I had built around my heart for years. I had responded to childhood injuries by raising a fortress around my heart brick by brick so life wouldn't hurt so badly. If only I had realized that the impenetrable walls only kept the pain *in.* I rarely cried, and whenever I did, I reminded myself not to let it happen again. *Hand me another brick.* I was an emotional shut-in. And I thought I was doing myself a favor.

My firstborn changed all that. Suddenly I had no defense. The walls came tumbling down, and my heart lay utterly exposed to human elements. A seven-pound, three-ounce "David" had slain my Goliath armor. Something had finally gotten to me. Totally vulnerable, I was terrified. I'm not sure I can articulate what I felt. Sometimes emotions simply defy explanation, but I felt that something outside of me finally had the ability to kill me—shatter me—for the precise reason that I was hopeless to *keep it* outside. She made it all the way in. My first experiences with unprotected love were excruciating. I don't know any other way to say it: love literally hurt. I would hold her in my arms and rock her for several hours at a time, and the tears would pour down my cheeks. I didn't know if I could stand the pain of loving something that much.

Our tendency is to wrap a wound as tightly as possible. This time, God's remedy was to take my wounded heart and *unwrap* it so it could get some air and begin to heal. Even when He binds our wounds, His bandages breathe. When God first began unwrapping my heart, the "nerve endings" felt so exposed that it seemed to throb instead of beat. I felt everything so vividly that I could hardly bear it. My second child was planned, and yet when I saw the "positive" indication on the pregnancy test, I sat in the bathroom floor and cried my eyes out. Why? Because I knew that a second creature was about to have the ability to slay me. I sobbed until it was out of my system, stood to my feet, brushed myself off, and valiantly thought something like, "Prepare to die." I was convinced that loving them would kill me, but I was certain of one thing above all else: they were worth it.

The point? They *haven't* killed me. *Yet,* that is. There's still time. The truth is, I don't think they're going to. Not because they are basically good kids. They have a lot of life ahead of them and all sorts of life-altering decisions yet to make. There's no guarantee they'll always make the best ones. I certainly didn't. Furthermore, my change of heart isn't because they are no longer as young and high risk. I understand from my friends that adult children can worry you and break your heart in ways younger children never could have dreamed. I have several reasons why I no longer think they're going to "kill" me. First of all, I have learned that pain doesn't kill.

I will never forget the jolt that tore through my soul with our son's departure. We had raised a close relative's son as our own for seven years, never realizing that God would plan for him to reenter his birth mother's life and home at age eleven. I threw my hands over my heart and fought like a Trojan not to give way to it. God gently pulled my hands away and said, "My child, go ahead and feel it. The pain will not kill you. It will be a reminder that you are very much alive, engaged, and that you loved with abandon. That was your primary assignment. Your present pain proves you did it." It was at this moment God spoke a transforming truth into my life: The goal of life is not the absence of pain. It's the presence of glory. God's glory. And sometimes that comes most vividly with pain. Not only have I learned that pain doesn't kill; I have learned that I will never lose or be betrayed by the one thing with absolute power to destroy me—God Himself. For nothing shall "separate us from the love of God that is in Christ Jesus our Lord" (Rom. 8:39).

Many losses came over that two-year period leading up to my first child's spring from the nest. Some of them were things I formerly believed my heart could not survive. It did. *I* did. Not only have I survived, I have beheld glimpses of glory I would not otherwise have seen, had pain not intensified my spiritual senses. I have accepted these truths for myself, but now it becomes my challenge to accept them regarding my children. Can I believe that pain will not kill them either? Do I want my children to see the glory of God? Can I trust that He will only use pain when nothing else will shed quite the same light on the face of Jesus Christ? And when it comes right down to it, is pain not an inevitable part of life for both the redeemed and the unredeemed? And can I at least be grateful that my children's will never be in vain . . . if they are willing to receive the vision? I'm not sure these are questions I can answer once and for all. They will challenge me afresh with every crumpled Kleenex of one kind or another that I'll discover along the way.

Oh, how we would shield our children if we could. Wouldn't we? Second only to the certainty of how terribly I would miss them, my most overwhelming emotion over their departure was fear. What would happen now that I would no longer be able to defend them from all the fire-breathing dragons in life? *As if I had been.* Among the ways you and I have been created in the image of our creator, His omnipotence doesn't happen to be one of them. Let's say it all together now: *We are not all-powerful.* God graciously forced me to come face-to-face with the fact that one of my biggest issues was the measurable amount of control I was about to lose over my children's lives.

True, one of our chief parental responsibilities is to provide healthy and reasonable protection for our children while still offering them room to grow. I didn't want to provide healthy and reasonable protection, however. I wanted *total* protection. The irony is that had I been able to provide some semblance of it, they would have needed protection *from me.* Ask any overprotected child. Their protector has inadvertently become their offender. We simply cannot take the risk of pain out of our loved ones' lives. If we tried our hardest to keep them sheltered from the pain of the outside world, it would simply avalanche from the inside. Trust me on this one: Dealing with pain from the outside is far easier than dealing with pain from the inside. Let's do our best to keep the enemy on the outside.

That crumpled Kleenex was a vivid reminder that something had breathed a little fire on my child that I knew nothing about. And it was just a token of times to come. Pain *will* come, welcomed or not. Problems will arise that I cannot fix. Some I will know about. Others I won't. What is my hope when they do? That my children will know *where to go:* straight to the throne of grace so that they may receive mercy and find grace to help them in their time of need (Heb. 4:16). And that they will know *what to do:* pour out their hearts to God for He is a refuge for them (Ps. 62:8). In other words, I hope they keep blowing their sweet noses and crumpling those Kleenexes right there at the edge of the throne of grace. When they hurt badly enough, *I hope they cry.* That's what healthy people do. God's Word never said we were not to grieve our losses. It says we are not to grieve as those who have no hope (1 Thess. 4:13). *Big difference.*

As our children begin to grow up, I think they need to know that it's still OK to cry. "Life" doesn't give us that permission. Perhaps parents should. Take it from someone who did her best to fasten a clamp on her emotions. Tears have great value. Not one tear that is poured out before God ever goes unnoticed . . . for indeed "Thou tellest my wanderings: put Thou my tears into Thy bottle: are they not in Thy book? When I cry unto thee, then shall mine enemies turn back: this I know; for God is with me" (Ps. 56:8–9 KJV). Over and over in His Word, God calls upon His children to cry to Him and cry *out* to Him. In fact, you will rarely find record of a great deliverance that He granted until they did. God not only gives His children permission to cry; He rather encourages it.

As long as I live, I will never be able to think about permission to cry without flashing back to the most tender scene I've witnessed between my daughters. After a two-and-a-half-year battle with cancer, my mother lay on her deathbed. Thankfully, it was the same bed she had slept in for many years. Surely in her discomfort, the sameness of her surroundings was of some comfort. Through events that could only have been orchestrated by a merciful God, my brother who was caring for her discerned a decline in her condition and called all of us to start heading home. He was somewhat reluctant to voice the SOS because of the distance involved and the reality that death can sometimes linger excruciatingly. In the course of the next twenty-four hours, all five of my mother's children, most of her sons and daughters-in-law and an entire litter of grandchildren gathered around her. She knew it all right. Most of my relatives share my rather enthusiastic personality. (Some might be more inclined to label it *obnoxious*.) Mom's last hours were anything but quiet. She had "shushed" us all of our lives, but we wouldn't have minded her at the last any more than we had minded her from the first.

I cannot imagine that she would have wanted it any other way. I recall a decade or so ago hearing a deep sadness in her voice as we visited on the phone. "Mom, what's the matter? You sound really down." I've replayed her response many times, particularly since the girls packed their bags for college. "I know this sounds silly, but I just wish I still had sixteen feet under the dining table." She was including her mother who lived with us until her own death, making a family of seven into a family of eight. Oh, what fun we often had crowded around that rickety old table. It was not only the dinner table. It was also the game table where we hooted and hollered so loud our voices could be heard across the county line. We certainly were not the poster family for functional, but we could put the *fun* into dysfunctional. As we all descended on her home several summers ago, we did not gather at the dining table where we always had. We gathered around her bed. Our "Queen of Everything" was dying.

Mom lived about a day and a half from the time my brother sounded his alarm. During those long hours we streamed in and out of the room. Amanda had asked me to please understand that she could not possibly go into Mom's room. She explained that her heart could not bear it, but she would sit in the next room and pray. I completely understood and would not have pressured her for anything. My only concern was that she not regret her decision later. I understood why she felt she could not take it. The two of them had the most precious relationship, just as my Mom had with all her grandchildren. But Mom made each one feel like her favorite. The two of them had bonded almost from birth. My mom stayed with me the week after Amanda was born, and Amanda's heartstrings were nearly as tied to her grandmother as they were to me. There I was trying my hardest to nurse while my mother was slipping her a bottle on the sly. I always teased that the only reason Amanda was closer to me is because I stayed when "Nanny" went home. I was the only "mom" she had left.

We don't need a child psychologist to analyze why my mother's grandchildren loved her so. She *played* with them. I'm quite sure she died with Play-Doh under her fingernails. I would find her and Amanda hiding in the closet together, giggling like a pair of little girls. They played dress up together. They spent endless hours in the toy aisle at Kmart. Once Melissa was born, Mom scooted Amanda to one knee and perched the new one on the other. They did everything together. They even lost their teeth about the same time. Mom was a good mother. But she was the best grandmother I have ever seen. How blessed they were.

Unfortunately, to the degree we love, we often grieve. Amanda's heart was broken not only by my mother's imminent death but by her scarred and emaciated body. Melissa's heart was broken too. Like yours, my children simply have very different temperaments. Melissa sat right there with Mom for hours on end telling her everything under the sun, even when the tiny patient responded little, if at all. Melissa hung on to her hand, laughing and crying intermittently. After a while, our hospice nurse hinted that the time was probably hastening. Melissa suddenly darted from the room and headed for her older sister. I didn't know the conversation that took place until it was told to me later.

"Amanda, you have to go in and see Nanny. I am scared you will be so sorry later if you don't."

"I can't, Melissa. I can't stand it. It will just *kill* me."

"Amanda, I'll go with you." Melissa reached out and took her hand.

"But, Melissa, I'm afraid I won't be able to keep from crying."

"SO? Cry!" Melissa responded. "Amanda, Nanny knows our hearts are broken. She knows that we love her too much to keep from crying. Go ahead and cry. She knows!"

Everyone else left the room but two teenage sisters and one dying grandmother. I stood outside the door and watched perhaps the most precious scene of my daughters' lives. They both knelt down right beside her bed and held her hands. She had held theirs so many times as they crossed the street. How fitting that they were there to hold hers as she prepared to cross the heavens. "Nanny, Amanda is here with me." My mother groaned tenderly and opened her eyes. I then heard a voice come from my oldest daughter that took me back nearly fifteen years. She sounded exactly as she did in preschool. "Hi, Nanny. It's me." Then she began to cry. Sob. Melissa held one of Nanny's hands and put her other arm around her big sister as she said, "It's OK." Both the girls cried. And then their Nanny did too. Oh, how she hated to leave her grandchildren behind. My girls spent some of my mother's last lucid moments with her. She did not fade into unconsciousness until she heard each one of them say, "Nanny, you are my best friend." She stared at their faces as hard as she could and through simple groans, she said something that neither girl could possibly have misunderstood. "And you are mine. *All of you.*"

I was so thankful I had already learned earlier that year that pain does not kill us. Otherwise, I would never have been able to stand in that doorway. My firstborn learned the same lesson that day. She is so like her mother. What a priceless moment we would have missed. Oh, what we forfeit when we deny our hearts the right to feel. Sometimes we protect ourselves from the most precious moments in life. I stood right there and watched my three best girls—my mom and my two daughters—double-tying their heartstrings one last time so the knot would hold fast until eternity. Before me was the chain of life. And I had had the blessed privilege of being the one who linked those beloved creatures—those very best friends—together.

Many a crumpled Kleenex gathered on the bedside table that day. They were not hidden under the edge of the bed. We cried openly . . . for we loved her so.

Now, that's more like it. When all
else fails, jump in the nearest pool.

CHAPTER 4

CLIFFSNOTES

My daughters are hilarious. In fact, my idea of a "night out with the girls" is to be with my own. A large part of what makes them so amusing is that they are total opposites to each other—even after all these years. How these two children came from the same womb is a complete mystery. Perhaps I have an undiagnosed multiple personality disorder that caused them to be birthed from two different mothers. One thing is sure. If they have two different moms, I'm both of them. I remember birthing them with astounding clarity. Frankly, they hurt. In fact, childbirth may have been the very moment my personality split. No matter what made them so different, they have finally grown to appreciate their dissimilarities. Not a moment too soon, I might add. Their mammoth differences caused no few conflicts growing up. Sharing the same bathroom with an alien from outer space (which each wholeheartedly considered the other) can be challenging.

My eldest placed a high value on personal space. My youngest didn't know there was such a thing. My eldest needed peace to function at her best. My youngest thrived on chaos. My eldest used words cautiously. My youngest used words . . . copiously. Having been called down in her fourth-grade class for excessive verbiage, she topped off her recount of the story to me by saying, "I'll just be honest with you, Mom. My new motto is 'Why be quiet when you can talk?'" Her motto has been repeated a thousand times in our home with great mirth. I love how God does that, don't you? He can take a tense family moment, treat it with time, and transform it into a thousand laughs.

One of the most pronounced differences between my girls has been their approach to schoolwork. If their polar attitudes in this regard had become mottos, one would have been "work for school" and the other would have been "make school work for you." I'll let you guess which belonged to which. School was very important to Amanda. She was a diligent student from the start, having loved nothing better than a book from the time she was a year old. She was the product of two bookworms, and her birthright turned into a love of knowledge. I will never forget her final day of first grade. She jumped off the school bus and ran to me waving her report card, yelling, *"I passed!"* Mind you, the child had received nothing but *E*s for *excellent* all year long, but were we ever relieved! Almost a decade and a half later, she hasn't changed all that dramatically. Even in college, she'd practically rather drop a class and take it again than get a *C*. Over and over her father and I have said, "There are some courses in college that are so far outside a person's realm of understanding, you make your goal to simply *pass* them." Not our Amanda. *Why bother taking it if I'm not going to pursue a good grade?* Uh . . . to graduate?

Amanda took every homework assignment seriously. She believed in pulling her own weight on group projects. She embraced the concept of actually studying for an exam. If backpack poundage is any indication of intelligence, she was brilliant. The thing threw my back out every time I handed it to her. Seventy-five pounds if it was an ounce. She was a teacher's kind of student. They taught and she learned. She knows more intricate facts about more subjects than anyone I know . . . except her father. They can get into discussions about rock formations and weather patterns that boggle the mind, while Melissa and I are content to remember the way to the mall. Don't get the idea Amanda is a boring child. This is no nerd. She is bright, funny, and fascinating! She simply loves to learn. And most of the time, her lessons "keep." She still conserves water and does her part for the ozone layer just like she was taught in her fourth-grade problem-solving class. And have I mentioned that she's never had a cavity? I'm not sure what dental prowess has to do with schoolwork, but somehow it all ties together. Melissa has had several cavities and could not care less about the ozone layer. Surely this is no coincidence.

Ordinarily, Amanda would rather have died than have gotten into trouble in class. I can, however, think of one exception. Perhaps you'll know where I'm going with all of this when I tell you that the closest bonding experience I ever remember my girls having is when Amanda finally brought home an *S* in conduct rather than an *E*. Amanda came running in the front door yelling, "Where is Melissa?" She was on the phone, of course, so Amanda headed upstairs to find her. Suddenly, the whole house began to shake as the two of them jumped up and down in great celebration, Melissa screaming, "I am *so* proud of you!" I have to admit all these years later, Keith and I were a tad proud of her too. She may have been one of the few college freshmen whose parents trusted them enough to say, "Loosen up on the schoolwork and have a good time!"

Trust me. Those were not the words we said to her sister. By and large, Melissa went to school for the social stimulation. Her very acceptable grades were a testimony that she may have been the smartest person in the house. After all, if she found time to study for a test, it was usually on the way to school. *While driving.* It had been impossible to find the time the night before between phone calls. And, anyway, virtually every single test the child ever took fell into the following category: "It's just not a test you can really study for, Mom." *I see.* All I have to say is, thank goodness for athletics. Melissa's chief motivation for passing her classes was maintaining the GPA required for playing sports. More often than not, *whatever works* was my parental philosophy. Keith and I made plenty of other mistakes, but we tried very hard to allow our girls the right to be different without differentiation. They never saw one another's report cards and were rewarded according to their obedience, not their performance. They each won my respect in different ways, and God protected my heart from partiality. I wouldn't have had a clue which one to prefer anyway!

Even though Melissa's academic philosophy varied from her sister's, she was never one to hate school. Most of the time, she was quite happy to go since that's where all the action was. Actually, she loved most of her teachers and in pure self-defense, most of them loved her too. To this day, almost every time I run into Melissa's former teachers, they grin a certain way when they ask me about her. The teachers who seemed the most mystified by my youngest never failed to have taught my eldest. Let me just put it this way: Amanda paved the way and Melissa plowed it up. The teachers that taught them both rarely missed an opportunity to tell me how different my girls were, to which I liked to respond as if they had handed me the most wonderful compliment. After all, I'm sure that's how they meant it.

If they could only see Melissa now. Today she really does allow her college professors to do the talking. She does her homework and even studies for tests. Who knows what will happen *tomorrow*, but that's what she's doing *today*. Yes, she's developing into a fine student, but she still doesn't like it. Just a few days ago I got really tickled when she told me of a recent conversation she had with the Lord. Melissa never says anything without passion, so "hear" it with proper enthusiasm:

"Mom, I was so sick of studying the other day that I just said to the Lord, 'Father, the wisdom of this earth is meaningless! Surely You would rather me learn Your Word than all this worldly wisdom. Just miraculously give me the knowledge to get me through the test and let me concentrate on more important things!'"

"What did He say?" I asked.

She quipped, "Baloney, Melissa. Get back to studying."

I howled. Perhaps you have a bit of trouble picturing God saying "Baloney." Thankfully, God can speak in whatever ways His children understand. Melissa understands baloney. So does her mother.

The true test is yet to come, however. Just how much her study habits have changed will surface the first time she has a lengthy and ever-so-outdated literature book to read and a subsequent essay to write. Melissa is the self-proclaimed *Queen of CliffsNotes.* Just to name a few of the feathers she left behind: CliffsNotes for *Jane Eyre, The Scarlet Letter, Hamlet, Madame Bovary.* You name it. She's got it. With a fair amount of confidence, I think I can also assure you that she read only a CliffsNotes version of the CliffsNotes. How did she still make good grades? I already told you. Melissa understands baloney. When she wrote an essay on a book, she simply expounded so verbosely on the little she knew, it sounded like a lot. Sounds familiar.

Every time I see that stack of CliffsNotes on her shelf, I think the same thing. We might get away with CliffsNotes versions of the old classics from time to time, but we will be terribly cheated and ill equipped for life if we rely on a CliffsNotes version of God's Word. I was raised on CliffsNotes. My guess is, you were too. Basically, isn't that what differentiates us into a variety of denominational beliefs? Our various CliffsNotes versions of Scripture? Without realizing it, sometimes we approach Scripture by reading only what we already believe. CliffsNotes. Please don't misunderstand me. I'm certainly not knocking religious denominations. I attend a denominational church that I love very much. Perhaps you do too. I am so grateful for all that my church and my denomination have taught me, but I believe our churches were never meant to be the sole source of our Bible knowledge. We are unwise to hold our churches and denominations responsible for teaching us absolutely *everything* we need to know about the Word of God. To me, that's a large part of what the "priesthood" of the individual means (1 Pet. 2:5, 9). Because Jesus Christ is our Great High Priest, not only can we *approach* God without a human "go-between," we can also *hear and learn from God* in some sacred moments without one.

Nothing could be further from my mind than forsaking the assembling of believers in our local churches. I am a very vocal advocate of attendance and involvement in the local church of our and God's choice. A friend of mine had a four-year-old granddaughter who coined an excellent rule of thumb for choosing a church. My friend had taken her to the Christmas pageant at our church. It is quite an extravaganza with an elaborate set, a very talented cast, and, much to the delight of the children, *live animals.* During one scene, the actor portraying Christ rode a donkey right down the aisle next to the little girl. In total ecstasy and amazement, she said, "Grandma, I didn't know Jesus went to *our* church!" There you go. The best possible grounds for choosing a church is making sure Jesus goes there. But even when He does, He may not get all the freedom He'd like from the pastor's pulpit and the teacher's podium. Time alone places limitations on what we can learn in our church services.

I'm simply suggesting that there may be more to learn from God and His Word than our different churches or denominations may teach us. Staying under a steady dose of teaching from the pulpit of my church is a necessity to me. It helps me grow and stay balanced, keeps me plugged in, and protects me with much-needed authority. However, I have also learned the tremendous value of seeking to know God through my own private study of His Word and through the materials of teachers and authors outside my church. Lean over here so I can whisper this part in your ear: Even *outside my denomination.* Don't tell a soul.

I love the body of Christ. I may not line up point by point on every line of doctrinal interpretation in some of the messages I hear or lessons I read, but I have so much to learn and rarely fail to be richly blessed! Sometimes I also realize that I am the one who is "off" in the interpretation. The first ten years of my ministry, I taught only that which *I* had been taught by human teachers in a very limited structure. I would not have dreamed of learning from anyone outside my church. Oh, what I missed! I was scared to death to learn anything outside my safe perimeters partially because I was scared to discover I might be wrong in my interpretation. Well, I *was* wrong,—on a number of things. Other things I discovered to be quite sound and came to believe in them twice as strongly. I am no longer nearly as scared to be wrong,—*or to admit it.* I make mistakes in interpretations more often than I wish and have to go back and redefine or rephrase them—but at least I took the risk of learning! God is teaching me to become more and more "teachable." To keep evolving. To keep taking the risk of learning something new . . . or *un*learning something old and off base. He graciously protects me from pride by going to extreme measures at times never to allow me to dream I've become some kind of expert.

Although God most assuredly wills that His children study Scripture thoroughly, scholarship is not His main goal for us. Relationship is. I feel the same way about *my* children.

Yes, their knowledge and understanding of our family principles and house rules are very important to me, but I am far more interested in a close and healthy relationship with them. The primary reason for the rules is so we can enjoy a *closer* and *healthier* relationship and Keith and I can trust them with blessing. When children honor their parents, parents can bless their children. The same concept is true of our fellowship with God, though we may not realize it. If we stick to a CliffsNotes version of God's Word, we could risk living our entire lives with the impression that the Bible is nothing more than a book of rules and regulations from a perfect God to a pitiful people. Actually, the Bible is a book about relationship. True, there are plenty of dos and don'ts, but their express purpose is to enhance relationship. There is so much to the Word! I want to learn all of it! Although I will never attain such a lofty goal in my earthly tenure, I want to take the example of the apostle Paul and spend my life pressing on toward the goal (Phil. 3:14).

Allow me to stomp my feet just a little bit while I make the next statement: I don't want to raise my children on CliffsNotes! I want them to know the whole counsel of the Word of God. I have chosen to raise my children in a denominational church, but I don't want to raise "denominational" children. I want to raise young women of the Word, who can in some way appreciate all *Christian* denominations even when they might not fully agree with them. Maybe I'm just naïve enough to think that is possible. I just hope I'm naïve enough to get away with it. I deeply want my children to be blessed by the whole body of Christ. Not just a slice of it. I also want my children to know the joy of worshiping and studying with Christians of other races and cultures. These kinds of attitudes and practices will not just develop in our children naturally. Not even in otherwise "good" kids. By nature, we are totally self-absorbed and nearsighted. A revolutionary change in our way of thinking is always radical and deliberate. If we parents want these kinds of views in our children, we are going to have to teach them overtly and live them outrightly.

One of the deepest pleas Christ made to His Father on the eve of the Crucifixion is that His followers would be one: "May they be brought to complete unity to let the world know that you sent me and have loved them even as you have loved me" (John 17:23). Unity unleashes such a powerful testimony that through it Christ said the world would know that God sent Him. What more profound influence could we possibly want? Christ is waiting for His bride, the church, to "make herself ready" (Rev. 19:7). One thing I know: Every man wants his woman to pull herself together. I think maybe that's what Jesus wants from His bride too.

Today when we hear such dismal news concerning America's youth, I have had the unspeakable privilege of getting to see glorious streams of light shining in the darkness. God is raising a generation of young followers with an astounding passion for Christ. Sure, their knowledge needs to grow to match their zeal, but in our attempt to teach them, let's not ruin them! And while we're at it, let's learn something from them. They don't have our hang-ups, and they don't want them. They aren't nearly as prone to label themselves by certain doctrines or denominations, so let's not help them. They want to *attend* church. They don't want to *pretend* church. They are begging us for authenticity. Thank goodness, they see *some* . . . but not nearly enough.

I believe their generation really has a potential for unity that mine—and those my senior—might not as readily enjoy. Let's join them. They want to be Christians who take part in church, not churchmen who take *part* of Christ. How do I know? Because two of them bring their laundry to my house on a regular basis. That same child with a shelf full of CliffsNotes has a Bible marked from Genesis to Revelation and visited half a dozen churches of various denominations in her college town before making *her* decision where to attend. Her big sister did the same thing. Don't think I'm not keeping an eye on them, but so far they don't appear to be wigging out. No, their generation may not have much appreciation for *Jane Eyre* and *Madame Bovary*, but I see a growing population of passionate believers who are crazy about Jesus Christ. No CliffsNotes versions for them. They want the unabridged edition. Who knows? They may be just the ones that teach us the number *one*.

Some kids are a handful.

Others are a whole arm full.

CHAPTER 5

THE BINDERS

Don't get the idea that Melissa's affinity for CliffsNotes meant she didn't care about her grades. On the contrary, several times throughout the school year, she would rededicate her life to scholastics somewhat like we rededicate our lives at my church after we've wandered from God. She simply walked the aisle at school.

Actually, Melissa's scholastic backsliding was a cycle that I finally learned to see coming. The sequence went like this: She would increasingly play around and have a good time until the ink on her social graph would peak so high, it would finally go off the page. I would start growing concerned. Her pat answer to my homework inquiries would be: "I don't have any." (Translation: "I'm not *doing* any.")

Next she would begin making comments about how unreasonable some of her teachers were. This particular signal was tantamount to black smoke coming from a volcano. The lava was bubbling. Prepare for the spew. It would always happen at night . . . the same way every time: She would hang up the phone about 10:00 P.M. and suddenly burst into tears. I would ask why. She would sob, "I am so stressed! I have a project due tomorrow, and *they* haven't given us a single chance to do it!" I always wanted to know who *they* were, but by this time it was too late. We were in full-blown crisis. Mount Vesuvius was erupting. The dogs would run under the bed. Keith would take his newspaper into a quieter place. I'll let you guess where.

Mothers are the only ones in the house who can still function while covered in lava. Soaked to the skin, I would usually offer my body to the flames and jump into the crisis with her. With every catch of my breath, I'd repeat the same question: "Why do you do this to yourself?" (Translation: "Why do you do this to *me?*") She would work like a maniac and squeak out the project by the skin of her teeth. After very few hours of sleep, the next morning she would pull out of the driveway and head to school in a cloud of volcanic ash, yelling something out of the window that sounded like, "Thank . . . love . . . sorry, Mom!" But the cycle wasn't over yet.

When Melissa got her grade, by the pure grace of God, the mark would invariably be quite adequate. But she knew she had far more than an "adequate" mind. The child knew good and well she could do much better. She could "get by" on what she was doing, but the fact was, she wasn't a "get by" kind of girl. In the wave of dissatisfaction with herself, she would make a firm resolution. *It was time for a fresh start.*

Every single fresh start began like this: She'd go straight to Eckerd Drugs and buy a brand-new binder that sounded nice and crispy when she opened it, and a package of brand-spanking-new-college-rule-notebook-paper. She'd march through the front door, clean all the trash out of her backpack, put her new paper in her new binder, stick a set of unused pens in the zipper bag, and announce, "There. I'm ready for a new start." Did it work? You better believe it! Gratefully, Melissa's spiral tended upward. That is exactly why my enthusiastic social butterfly was able to wing her flight to a fine college after all the playing she had done.

We have done a heap of cleaning in Melissa's cluttered closet since she left for college, but there are a few things I cannot bring myself to throw away: at least twenty-five binders. I can't do it. I just cannot throw away that many fresh starts. I am utterly convinced that they were responsible for her ultimate success in school. She was willing to keep starting over until she learned to start getting it right. Perhaps you know me better than to think that I am holding on to those binders because they represent scholastic success in my child. No way. They represent something far more important than that.

Children have to know they can make a clean start. If they don't, I am utterly convinced they will not be whole adults. Somewhere along the way, failure, which I'll define as failure to measure up, *will* come. It's a fact of life. Whether we feel we've failed ourselves, others, or God, we all have a head-on collision with varying degrees of it throughout our lives. Children need to know how to deal with life when they let themselves down. If they can't get over it and make a new start, what in the world are they to do? Will they be twelve or fourteen years old with the best years of their life behind them? God forbid. Imagine the hopelessness of that kind of unspoken mentality. Sadly, it happens all the time. There *is* another way. We can view failure as an opportunity to develop a necessary life skill. After all, we'd be worse than failures without it. We'd be merciless egomaniacs. Failure is one of life's most powerful teachers. We will all sign up for its class at one time or another, but we can each decide whether or not to pass the course. How we handle our failure to measure up determines whether we're going to simply "get by" in life or "press on." Surely something down deep inside our souls tells us we were never meant to just "get by."

My concept of the parent-child relationship we share with God has changed dramatically through my own years of parenting. To some extent, I've come to believe that proverbial "good kids" are often in the eye of the beholder. In other words, what I might consider a "good kid" might not at all be your definition. As you first began to read this book, you might have been tempted to think, *I could be a happy mom, too, if I had such good kids.* Hear my heart: they *are* good kids . . . who have at times made some bad decisions. Not unlike their parents. And grandparents. And great-grandparents. If I told you a few of the decisions these "good kids" have made, you might gasp and revoke their "good" crown. Yet, to me, they aren't just good kids. They are great kids. Not because they've done everything right, but because when they did something wrong, sooner or later they mourned it, repented, took responsibility, turned it over to the Lord, and committed to a fresh start. *A little wiser.* At the risk of making a slightly shocking confession, it was as important to me that my children be no more self-righteous than they were *un*righteous. In His Gospels, Christ seemed far more tolerant of a repentant sinner than a self-righteous, self-proclaimed saint. For this moment the girls appear to be neither self-righteous nor unrighteous. No small feat for any of us, in my opinion. Such a delicate balance certainly didn't come accidentally, nor is it easily maintained. For now, I believe what is helping them keep their carts between both of those ditches is that according to their own standards and in their own estimations, they have each found themselves sitting in *Failure's* class. They listened, they chose to be good students, and they passed the course. Their diploma was a new binder and a fresh package of notebook paper awarded by a very wise and merciful Principal. A clean start. There's nothing like it.

I am far from an expert on children. Anything I've learned has come either from having children or being one of God's. I don't know much, but I know that children have to be released from past mistakes. Life bulges with burdens of mistakes. Somewhere along the way they've got to be able to lay down the old bag before they start collecting a new one. Double baggers are miserable people. Guilt heaped upon guilt becomes too much to bear. No doubt, parents have to discipline and deal wisely with poor choices their children make, but when it's over, it's got to be over. That's God's way.

Psalm 130:3–4 says, "If you, O LORD, kept a record of sins, / O Lord, who could stand? / But with you there is forgiveness; / therefore you are feared." Did you catch how the verse ended? I think sometimes we fear that if we are forgiving, our children will not respect us. When we recognize God's unwavering standard yet realize He has completely forgiven us for our sins, we are awed. The same is often true of our children. When they are forgiven by parents who set an example of righteousness—though certainly not of perfection—they will regard the gift of grace far more highly. Their realization that the wrong was forgiven though the standard was not lowered will often have a serious impact.

Parents who shame their children with constant reminders of past mistakes can be the most destructive force in a child's life. Shame is Satan's "Gotcha!" Not God's. Unfortunately, shaming parents often inadvertently give their children a similar view of God, the ultimate authority figure. If perchance the shamed child *does* end up pursuing a relationship with God, it is often motivated by guilt, displacing the rich, liberating relationship that was meant for him or her. The truth is, God sent His Son to endure the unimaginable shame of the cross precisely so we could be delivered from it. He who "scorned the shame" two thousand years ago *still does.* Shame is never His game.

God is the perfect role model for imperfect parents. He keeps a close eye on His children and knows they have sinned long before they confess it. Through the power of His Holy Spirit, He begins wooing them. He waits and He waits until they can't resist telling Him. The millisecond they cry out in repentance, He forgives them. "As a father has compassion on his children, / so the LORD has compassion on those who fear him; / for he knows how we are formed, / he remembers that we are dust" (Ps. 103:13–14). Search the lives of Abraham, Moses, David, Peter, and Paul, and savor the reality that God's children cannot outsin His ability to forgive them. God has mercy on His children "according to His loving kindness" (Ps. 51:1). That means He is never unbiased about one of His own. He will never choose to set aside His love for us in order to make a purely "objective" decision. If chastisement is necessary for the child to learn, He assigns it, but even His discipline is biased by love. The Lord chastens those He loves as sons (Heb. 12:6). Never unnecessarily. Never unfairly. Never without full intention of benefit. Once God has forgiven the sin, He chooses to forget it. First Corinthians 13:5 says God's kind of love "keeps no record of wrongs." In other words, we get a new binder every time we truly repent and agree to a fresh start.

I have no idea where I would be if I didn't believe in fresh starts. I have little doubt my home would be in shambles, my life would be in a pit, and I most assuredly would not be in ministry. God has had much mercy in my life. Not shaming mercy but loving mercy. His kindness led me to repentance (Rom. 2:4). One way I can show Him my gratitude is to be merciful to others. Not foolish. *Merciful.* I also know for a fact that new beginnings really can work. Like Melissa and her scholastic "cycle," I lived much of my personal life in a cycle. I would grow increasingly out of control, wander too close to a pit, and fall in. Because I really did have a heart for God, albeit unhealthy, I would grow utterly miserable in that pit and, sooner or later, sorrow over sin would consume me. I would cry out to God, and He would faithfully pull me out of the pit. Because I did not understand the concept of His desire to be the all-surpassing power in my fragile jar of clay, I would try my hardest to be good for as long as I could. I was such an emotional wreck that the unhealthiness of my heart would finally exceed my determination . . . then I'd head right back for trouble.

Oh, the patience of God who kept reaching out to me like a parent reaches out to a one-year-old taking his first few steps. I would fall and cry. He would set me back on my feet.

Little by little, I began to learn. How wise we are to realize that living "rightly" is a *learned* behavior (Isa. 1:16–17; 26:9–10). God slowly opened my eyes to see my pitiful tendencies, reassuring me continually of His unfailing love. In His wise counsel, He also allowed me to suffer enough consequences to finally agree to whatever freedom required. After many second chances, I finally learned to walk. Oh, nowhere close to perfection! But in victory. In the power of His Spirit. In the liberty of His truth. His willingness to never withhold a new beginning from me *worked*. That's why I dare not withhold one from *my* children.

It's been awhile since I looked at life from the bottom of a pit but not so long that I don't remember it well. I have no idea what is ahead for me. I pray desperately that I will make wise decisions, but the day I don't, fresh mercies will await me. For they indeed never cease. They are new every morning. Great is His faithfulness. I also have no idea what is ahead for my children. They are still young. They have many decisions ahead to make. I can't imagine theirs will *always* be wise ones. But in the image of my Father, I am challenged to have a fresh heap of mercy ready and waiting. When I'm dry, frustrated, and weary, thankfully, I can borrow a bucket full of His. I *must*, no matter how hard the prospect, because my children are watching for me to practice what I have preached of God.

I love to journal my prayers. It has been my practice for years. Like Melissa's, my closet is full of old spiral notebooks, but mine are written records of bits and pieces of my journey with God. Also like Melissa, when I get to the end of one, I run to that same Eckerd Drugs for another. I love few things better than a brand-new spiral notebook full of bright white paper. I never fail to meditate on it for a few minutes before I begin to write. I always wonder what will be ahead and what kind of "record" will fill those pages. Not a spotless one, that's for sure. But an honest one. Somehow as I record my frailties, my confessions, my petitions, and my cries for help, I am not discouraged. For I know that at the end of that journal is a new one. A clean white page. A fresh new start. A chance to do a little bit better than the last. To keep cooperating with God and to occasionally hear Him say, "Hang in there, sweet child. You are making so much progress."

A year or so ago, I sat in my closet and began looking through those old journals. I came to one that was only half-filled with writings. My usual practice is to write in my notebooks until the very last page, so I found the sudden cessation curious. Then I began to read. My heart ached as I read the record of such a painful time. The tears stung in my eyes as I recalled all the emotions and misery. Then I realized why I had stopped in the middle. On a hunch I picked up the next journal, and sure enough it began where the previous journal stopped. I had simply needed a new start. A fresh journal. A clean page. And I knew my God well enough to know He would give it to me. Thank goodness. All of us need a new binder from time to time.

At home in 1985.

Looking for "Paul" in all the
right places, Greek Islands, 1998.

CHAPTER 6

THE INDEX CARDS

I'm always looking for something. And I'm always finding what I'm not looking for. Simple-minded soul that I am, I invariably become so enthralled by what I'm *not* looking for, that I forget what I *am* looking for. Recently I wasn't looking for a drawer full of index cards. I was quite excited, however, when that's what I found. I'd been wondering where they were. I had looked for them a few months back but found something else. Then I forgot I was looking for them. I was so glad I was looking for something else a few days ago. Otherwise, I never would have found them.

These weren't just *any* index cards. A Scripture was written in permanent marker in my handwriting on each one. Surrounding the Scripture was each of our signatures. I clearly recalled what had prompted those Scripture cards and, true to form, I ceased my original search and took a trip down memory lane back to a simpler, if more exhausting, time.

Getting my children's somewhat undivided—albeit brief—attention to teach them the important things in life was so much easier when they were little. Like all children, they were filled with wonder, and since God is a master at supplying it (indeed, His very name is *Wonderful*), there were no few opportunities to give Him credit. Anything would do. A ladybug on a tree trunk. A delicate butterfly. Animal-shaped clouds to guess out loud. Rain. Sunshine. Rainbows. Lightning. Thunder. Wind. Leaves turning colors in autumn. Night-lights at bedtime. Sore throats. Ear infections. Quarrels over toys. Trips to the doctor. Yucky shots. With little effort God could be woven into any conversation. After all, the Author of life never writes a page we can't find Him on if we're looking.

My parents lived exactly an hour and forty-five minutes from our front door, and I could teach my children about God all the way there and back if I had the disposition. They sat in car seats nice and high where the view was sublime. The country roads gave us ample opportunity to talk about how God feeds the mama cow and how God created the mama cow to feed her calf. How a pony learns to walk just after it's born. How mud makes pigs happy. How wildflowers grow in the field and nobody picks them. How God can be the best friend of an elderly man sitting all alone on his porch. How God had too many good ideas to make us all the same color. Then when we were talked out, we could sing at the top of our lungs with our children's praise tapes. Precious moments. Teaching moments. I didn't always seize them. But when I did, I sensed the smile of God. Day in and day out, He was life. The center of a hundred conversations. Simple and spontaneous. No time for dissertations. A mom of young children must catch while catch can.

Their little minds had a thousand hands reaching and grabbing for everything they could see (not unlike their *physical* hands). A parent-teacher's job is to guide as much as possible what the hands of their minds grab and store. The marvel is that what they store cannot be stolen from them. The original meaning of the oft-quoted Proverbs 22:6: "Train a child in the way he should go, / and when he is old he will not turn from it," is not so much a guarantee that the child will grow to be godly as it is a promise that he cannot delete the truth that has been programmed into him. I like to translate it this way: If he turns from it, may it drive him crazy until it drives him to Christ. When children are little, they do not have to be chided into faith. They believe with ease. They delight to learn. And for the little while they do, let's delight to *teach!* We have a window of opportunity only until they start processing the avalanching stimuli of the world more independently. Our goal is that, by that time, they will have developed desirable habits for processing information.

Parent-teachers. That's what God has called us to be. God does not commission all parents to homeschool their children academically, but He most assuredly calls us all to homeschool our children *spiritually*. Not as a substitute for Sunday school and church but as the absolute foundation upon which other forms of spiritual encouragement build. Organized "church" was meant to be supplemental to the foundations poured by the parents. That's why it's so critical that parents have their own active and engaging relationship with God and know Him through His Word. God didn't assign the spiritual upbringing of children to churches or Christian schools. He assigned it to parents.

Deuteronomy 6:5–7 says, "Love the LORD your God with all your heart and with all your soul and with all your strength. These commandments that I give you today are to be upon your hearts. Impress them on your children. Talk about them when you sit at home and when you walk along the road, when you lie down and when you get up."

I don't think Scripture is suggesting a legalistic and awkward insertion of God-talk into every conversation. God's deepest desire is that we recognize that He *is* life and that no category of living is outside His realm of dominion or interest. "In Him was life, and that life was the light of men" (John 1:4). In other words, God Himself is what enlightens understanding about everything else in life. Knowledge about any subject is fragmentary without the enlightenment that comes from His relationship to it. Don't get me wrong. I don't think God is insisting upon showing up in every sentence that comes from a parent's mouth. He's talking about a human lifestyle that perpetually involves Him since God has graciously chosen to involve humans in life.

What is the key to this practice becoming completely natural to us? Oh, how wise our God! He prefaced His instruction to parents in Deuteronomy 6 with the perfect key: "Love the LORD your God with all your heart and with all your soul and with all your strength." When we develop an authentic love relationship with God, we will not be able to keep Him compartmentalized in "churchy," religious categories. Keith and the girls come up naturally in many of my conversations during the day. They come up in my writing. They come up in my speaking. I don't plan it. I can't *help* it. They come up naturally because they are part of who I am. I don't have to force them to fit. I consider them in every decision I make. They are always on my mind, either primarily or secondarily. Why? For the same reason your family is. Because I *love* them.

Love is key to anyone becoming part of everything we do. I believe God also has a second reason why love for Him is the critical foundation from which a parent teaches His precepts and commands: Love tempers everything—His love for us and our love for Him. Children are very perceptive. They can sense in us our affection or lack of affection for God. They will base much of their own choice to accept or reject a relationship with God on what they perceive in our hearts and attitudes, not just our words. They are reaching deep inside us with the hands of their minds trying to grasp how *we* feel about Him. How *do* we feel about Him? Often, the same way *our* parents did. What a needless tragedy that some of us grow up having known God only as the Big Bad Wolf. The Big Meanie in the Sky. The one parents use to threaten their children when they're at wit's end. The one who will "get" us when we're bad. If that's all we were taught and all we are teaching of God, we have missed Him almost entirely.

God is driven by *love*. That's what He *is*. Unlike us, He never acts contrary to who He is. Even in judgment or chastisement, God never ceases to love. I don't mind being told what to do nearly as much when the instruction comes from someone who loves me so lavishly that He was willing to make an unimaginable sacrifice. I also don't mind taking instruction from someone who doesn't demand to be obeyed for obedience's sake. Rather, He gives me certain regulations for living for my own good (Deut. 10:13). Certainly, I have been reprimanded and disciplined by God more times than I'd like to recall, but chastisement is not what has marked our relationship.

I'll tell you what has marked our relationship more than anything. I have found God to be a blast. I'm crazy about Him. I have so deeply enjoyed Him that I wanted few things more than for my children to enjoy Him too. I believe we've been created to do two things above all others: glorify God and thoroughly enjoy God. Every rule and regulation He gives is to prompt those two things. Yes, we were created for His holy pleasure, but we will ultimately—if not immediately—find much pleasure in *His* pleasure.

All of these concepts are braided together beautifully in John 15:9–11. Listen to them fall like rain on dry ground from the mouth of Christ: "As the Father has loved me, so have I loved you. Now remain in my love. If you obey my commands, you will remain in my love, just as I have obeyed my Father's commands and remain in his love. I have told you this so that my joy may be in you and that your joy may be complete."

Healthy young children are given to joy. It's a natural stimulus to them. The hands of their minds are constantly grabbing for it. Our children are searching to see if Christ's joy is in us. If they find it, they are far more likely to reach out and grab Him for themselves.

The older children get, the bigger their world grows. The bigger their world grows, the more there is for the thousand hands of their minds to grab. Hence, the index cards. You thought I had forgotten I found them, didn't you? Let me explain how our Scripture cards *happened*. By the time my children reached middle school, life grew far more complicated. Many other adults and peers had the opportunity to program information into my children's minds. We can't just raise our children in a vacuum. Sooner or later, they've got to discover life in the big world. I believe our primary task is to train them to constantly discover the *God of life* in the big world by slowly, carefully, and progressively broadening the boundaries.

I don't know about you, but I wasn't ready for all the competition that came with my children's broadened boundaries. That's because I didn't really have a crystal-clear paradigm for how I wanted to teach and parent. I appreciated many of the ways I had been raised, but I was trying to forge my own trail. I was unprepared for all the surprises. The increasing ages of my children brought many! Suddenly we had tons more homework and tons more activities. Sports, clubs at school, student council, and an ever-widening social circle, to name a few. Although our family prayed together many times, I had a difficult time managing what many Christian family experts call a daily "family altar time." Particularly by the time my children reached high school, our family members rarely seemed to be home at the same time. Further complicating matters, I also was challenged—like many of you—to find a delicate balance in my spiritual role in the home. My husband was a church-attending believer who often prayed with us and conversed about God, but he did not share some of the same lifestyle convictions. Nor did he desire to take a strong spiritual role.

What's a woman to do? I began to ask God that very question. He supplied an answer that I'm certainly not suggesting is *the* answer. It was simply a plan that helped the Moores in our dilemma. Please hear me say that the best possible plan is consistent family altar time. I knew that wouldn't happen at our house. We often prayed together as a family but not nearly often enough to equip our family for all we were facing "out there." I felt strongly that something "daily" needed to happen. But how? Our days all began and ended at different times. God heard my cry for help and started to unfold the plan. This was the thought process He brought to me: While we were rarely all at home and available at the exactly the same time, every single one of us was home early in the morning. Everyone could seek God "first" in the morning, even if our "firsts" were all at different times.

I awakened first. I had my own personal time with God before the family arose so I could be prepared for the day. I asked God every single morning to supply me with a Scripture for the day for our family. One that each of us could in some way comprehend. He never failed to be faithful since there are few things He wants to do more than equip His people with His Word. I wrote the Scripture on an index card then placed it on our hearth with an open and currently dated prayer journal where they could record any requests. A family devotional book also lay open for them to read that day's entry. At first my children said exactly what most would say: "How will we ever have time to do that in the morning?" I *joyfully* reminded them of a revolutionary truth from Matthew 6:33: "Children, do you realize that God says if we will seek Him first every day, all the other things in our day will fall into place?" I also assured them that I was not asking something unreasonable from them. They could literally accomplish what I was asking in five concentrated minutes—but those five minutes would transform their day if they would let them.

The plan worked. That's how I knew it had to be God's! Each family member was to come directly to the altar soon after getting out of bed. Each person's "first thing in the morning" worked well for us because we got up at different times. Amanda's day began before Melissa's. She was instructed to come downstairs, kneel at our little family altar, read the one- or two-minute devotional, hopefully pray for a few minutes, record any prayer requests in the journal, read our Scripture for the day, and sign her name on the index card as having completed the instruction. She would already find my name signed on the card because I arose first. (*Authenticity*—not requiring something of our children that we do not do.) Melissa did the same, and while Michael was still in our home, he did the same. I simply supplied several devotional books to fit their needs and reading levels.

With God's help I was able to do every single bit of this without undermining my husband's authority. He certainly wasn't *against* the plan. He thoroughly approved. He just didn't always participate. Sometimes Keith followed suit and his signature would be the last one on the card. Other times he didn't. That was OK too. I didn't require it of my husband because I am not his boss. I am, however, one of my childrens'!

Did they absorb any of it? You bet they did! True, some-times they would be out of sorts and in a contrary mood, lessening its effectiveness. Other times they may have been too sleepy to take it all in or perhaps one didn't feel well. And, certainly there were times they may have been too distracted to pay close attention, but some of it stuck! That I *know!* My children were somewhat like our bird dog, Beenie. Like all good bird dogs, Beenie has droopy lips. Her funny lips just don't make a tight seal. We practically have to put her outside to drink her water because almost as much splashes out of her mouth as slides down her throat. She's also the messiest eater you've ever seen, but her healthy frame testifies that some of the food makes it down. I believe the same concept is true of our children. Like most juveniles, my kids were pretty messy eaters and drinkers of the Word and the things of God. I'm sure there were some mornings when their lips were so "droopy" as much splashed out as slid in. Some of it "made it in," though. And whatever "made it in" will not return void. We've got God's word on it (Isa. 55:11). I must trust God that many of the things Michael was taught stuck to his ribs, but I see constant evidence that many of them stuck to the girls'.

My daughters are virtually grown. They don't live routinely under my roof anymore. I no longer have the constant opportunity to enjoy God with them, show them His works, and teach them His ways. Sure, there are still things to teach and demonstrate but the prime time for influencing what is poured into their spongelike minds has come and gone. My window has closed. But I can still watch them through it.

For the girls those five harried minutes first thing in the morning have turned into much more. For this season each has made it her practice to have a daily quiet time with God.

They no longer have a mother insisting on it. They're on their own. They don't always keep their appointments with God, but each of them tells me that when they don't, they *feel* it. Thank you, Holy Spirit. They talk about God just like they talk about any other primary love of their lives. He is the center of much of their activity. They are not yet entirely sure what they want to do with their lives, but they are certain of this: they want lives with *purpose*. They want to fulfill God's personal plan for them. I don't believe they will ever be satisfied to settle for less.

I look back upon the whole child-raising process now with total awe and wonder. I really didn't have a clue what I was doing. Had I really understood the life-altering power parents have to *help* or to *hinder*, it would have scared me half to death. I'm so thankful God knew what *He* was doing. I made so many mistakes. I missed so many cues. I didn't always seize golden opportunities. Sometimes I was so exhausted at their bedtimes that our nighttime prayers were pitifully brief, but to the grace of God, what we *did* sincerely attempt in His name *worked*.

In retrospect I am utterly convinced that the most powerful key to positively influencing my children came through something I sought not for them, but for me. I came to a place in my life where I wanted—more than anything else in the whole world—to love God. As a woman in my mid-twenties, I met someone who really *did* have a romance with God. Then I knew without a doubt it was possible, not just religiously hypothetical. I told God over and over that I wanted to love Him "like that." He whispered two words into my spirit that totally transformed my life. Two words that I have shared many times in my messages: *Pray to.* And I did. Over and over and over. With utmost sincerity. I still pray to love Him more than I pray for blessing, health, power, strength, or answered prayer. It is my soul's chief desire. All I know to say is that God graciously answered my prayer—just as He does every prayer that is offered in His will. Through countless mistakes a parent inevitably makes, the children knew I loved Him. And love covers a multitude of sins. More importantly to our children, love for God becomes their inheritance . . . *if* they are willing to receive it. "The LORD your God will circumcise your hearts *and the hearts of your descendants,* so that you may love him with all your heart and with all your soul, and live" (Deut. 30:6, emphasis mine).

God is so inconceivably good. He's not looking for perfection. He already saw it in Christ. He's looking for affection. That's why every lasting change in every home will invariably be a change of heart. Somehow He leads us to our God-ordained destinations—even when the road trip isn't pretty—if we truly have a heart for Him. He'll even supply the heart if we'll ask Him.

I'm always looking for something. And I'm always finding what I'm not looking for . . . except when I'm looking for Christ. Then I always find much more. I'm so glad I wasn't looking for those index cards that day. Their welcome intrusion in my search for something else reminded me that God can take the most meager effort and make it magnanimous. Our family signed our names on God's Word, and He signed His Word on our hearts. Isn't that just like Him? He'll outdo us every time. Dear, dear parent, don't grow weary in well-doing even if you think it's having little effect. Our labor in Him is never in vain. You'll see. Work while your "window" is open. Work with love, authenticity, and enthusiasm! Then when it closes, just keep looking through it. One day you'll see.

"You will seek me and find me when you seek me with all your heart . . ."
JEREMIAH 29:13

Amanda,
ever one to stop and smell the roses.

CHAPTER 7

THE ROSES

By the time both our daughters were in high school, we were fully immersed in Girl World. I no longer had a boy of my own in the home; however, we were rarely lacking in male company. Girl World has a magnetic attraction for Guy World. Both of our girls were cuter than "a ten-pound sack o' taters," as my people would say, so we had no few male suitors. Thankfully, the girls had pretty fair taste, so they rarely invited anyone to our home that I couldn't tolerate. Keith did not share my sentiments. They never introduced him to a single one he *could* tolerate. Don't get the wrong idea. These were fine young men. Keith is just . . . well . . . *Keith*. Let's see if I can explain.

I grew up in Arkansas. I have lived in Texas since I was fifteen years old, but I still cannot think like a *real* Texan. They are their own breed. And if Texans are their own breed, Keith is a *full* breed. That means his parents, grandparents, and great-grandparents were all native Texans. In fact, he tells me that his family has been in Texas since before the Civil War. I wish I could describe the look on his face and the pride in his voice when he tells me that. He almost gets tears in his eyes . . . and would, indeed, if it were more manly. Whatever you picture a

Texan to be, that's what I married. I didn't realize at the time how lucky I was that he lost control of his heart and walked the aisle with a foreigner. To Keith, the world ends at the state line. He insisted on state colleges for both girls because "what if they marry someone who will take them out of Texas?" Don't the Texas Rangers handle heinous crimes of that nature? Actually, I don't mind Keith's determination to see them settle in Texas so much since it appears that I'm planted here 'neath the mesquite trees until God delivers me to His heavenly kingdom. I'd just as soon my grandchildren do the same.

I can't say that all Texas men fit the description I am about to share with you. Those like Keith, however, would argue that all *true* Texans do. They either wear cowboy boots or they're embarrassed that they don't. They would rather die than wear sandals, no matter how rough the leather. Their hands are callused even if they work indoors. Why? Because they play *outdoors*. And their play is hard work. They are convinced Psalm 8:4–8 was written just for them: "What is man that you are mindful of him, / the son of man that you care for him? / You made him a little lower than the heavenly beings . . ." (They take the latter part very seriously.) " . . . and crowned him with glory and honor." (Their "crown" looks suspiciously like a cowboy hat.) "You made him ruler over the works of your hands; / you put everything under his feet." (They might tell you that the Hebrew translation of *feet* is "boots." You also wouldn't believe what they can get *under* them.) ". . . all flocks and herds, / and the beasts of the field, / the birds of the air, / and the fish of the sea, / all that swim the paths of the seas." Translation? They hunt and fish or wish they did. "It's *biblical*," Keith tells me.

What does all this have to do with male suitors? Everything. Once the girls reached high school, Keith developed the most peculiar behavior. Every time a young man visited one of our daughters, Keith was suddenly compelled to clean his shotguns. No, I'm not kidding. Don't get too nervous. The boys weren't in *terrible* danger. He was very careful to take them completely apart and lay them on the coffee table where he buffed and shined them up piece by piece. (The shotguns, not the male suitors.)

Since we only have one family room, the young men were forced to sit right across from "Mr. Moore" and wait an eternity for their date. Keith was never horribly rude or unfriendly. You don't have to be when you're cleaning shotguns. I assure you that it was rare for a young man to risk having one of Mr. Moore's daughters out beyond the promised hour. I think they knew he'd had ample time to get the shotgun reassembled. (Lest my man take exception to what I'm saying, let me clarify that he is a fanatic about gun safety.) They certainly knew he could hit a target because of the deer trophy displayed prominently on the wall.

Keith declares he had no idea he had descended to such tactics until we pointed out the astounding correlation between the girls' dates and his gun-cleaning habits. For a brief time he really tried to do better. He practiced casting his fishing lures in the family room instead. A four-pronged hook whizzing past a young man's ear is not nearly as intimidating as sitting within a foot of a double-barrel shotgun. I'll just put it this way: A young man had to *really* want to date one of our daughters.

Somehow they still managed. Several even persevered until Keith said more than three words to them. ("Who are you?")

A few young men did the unimaginable and actually grew on him, but don't get the idea he ever shared his bean dip with them or anything. One thing I knew for sure. If they were will-ing to deal with Mr. Moore, they had kind intentions toward our daughters. Some liked the girls enough to risk life and limb by showing up at the front door with flowers. Such an overt display of endearment completely baffled Keith. He didn't know whether to think they were being respectful or forward. When I heard him making a sound like a horse blowing its lips, I always assumed a young man had shown up with a bou-quet. I, of course, had to compensate for Keith's lack of appre-ciation. I would gush profusely and offer to put them in water. I then would yell something upstairs like, "Just wait until you see what a nice surprise this young man has for you. Why don't you *hurry* right down and see them?" Emphasis on *hurry*.

I remember once standing in the kitchen trimming the stems of a dozen red roses. Somehow *that* display of endear-ment was almost too much even for me. As I trimmed each one and put it in the vase, so many thoughts swirled through my mind. I didn't think my child was in love at that time, but I knew she was plenty old enough to feel the real thing. It was just a matter of time until each of my girls would give her heart away. As I carefully managed my way around the thorns, I thought how much true love hurts. *Pierces.* Even at its best. How it complicates life. What a risk it can be. Still, after I arranged all twelve roses in the vase and surrounded them with babies' breath, I stood back and marveled at the incredible beauty. Nothing so delicate . . . so perfect . . . as a deep crimson rose—nor what it represents in any language. I would not wish my daughters free of the risk and the complexity of cupid love for anything. In time. In God's plan. I believe in romance.

Romance. Not fairy tales. There's nothing like love to awaken a soul to the realization that if fairies *did* exist, they told a serious *tale*. Cinderella soon discovered that Prince Charming could smell a lot like his horse. Snow White sometimes thought she'd rather go home to the seven dwarves. Rapunzel found herself wishing she'd had a crew cut. The princess who kissed the frog recognized some of the same warts on her prince. Love tends to be blind only in the beginning. How else would we take the risk? Oh, but love *is* worth the risk when our hearts belong to God.

Human love is always imperfect love, but God has sentimentally chosen to whisper hints of the perfect through its imperfections. Through the flawed, He kindles faith for the flawless, awakening the mortal heart to a brush with the immortal. Such love suggests that there is still stuff of heaven falling to earth. For true love is by its nature selfless, sacrificial . . . and there is nothing in the heart of man so divine. It is a gift of God . . . even at times graced upon the godless to bear His witness. To have fallen in love hints to our hearts that all of earthly life is not hopelessly fallen. Love is the laughter of God.

The love between a man and a woman is like the intimately and mysteriously closed hand of God held behind His back. He watches for moments to stretch forth His hand and unfold a grand surprise. These are some of life's more perfect moments. Love breaks the cynic's heart and unmasks the façade of the most mature, leaving its captives jumping up and down like children. We can control ourselves through anger and rage far more masterfully than love. Love is a master. Divine love is *our* Master. Indeed, the marriage of two so diverse yet overtaken by love is exactly what God created and ordained to give glimpse to the eternal future of the redeemed. God is a romantic. Remove the romance from the Word, and all you have left is rules and regulations. The *Law*. I'll pass. I want the real thing. Let it slay me.

Keith and I have certainly not lived a fairy tale. Both our hearts were so scarred by life that neither of us had a clue how to love. We fought like cats and dogs, and each was so miserable at times that we felt we could not bear it. There were seasons when we felt absolutely no love toward one another. At times we were certain that life—or the other person—had finally killed whatever affection we had. But that's the thing about God. He can resurrect the dead. He *alone* can resurrect the dead. I have no clue how couples without Him quicken to love again after death of heart. It takes something divine to roll the stone away and call a Lazarus relationship back from the dead. It takes *forgiveness*. A celestial trait invading a terrestrial heart. Love is just lust until it has been seasoned by time and refined by forgiveness. God created life and knows what makes it work. Therefore, He insists on two things above all else: that we love as we've been loved (John 15:12) . . . and that we forgive as we've been forgiven (Eph. 4:32). In other words, "I have poured My life into you. Dip into the deepest well and offer another a drink."

Not just once. And not just in the crises. But as a practice. In the little things before they get to be big things. In the big things so we can go back once again to the little things. God calls upon the loved not just to love but to be loving. God calls upon the forgiven not just to forgive but to be forgiving. These are the things that cause our lives to bear the very witness of God because they are beyond man. Boy, have Keith and I done a lot of forgiving. And don't get the idea that I have done more than he. Marriage has been hard for both of us, but nothing has shown us the sustaining power of God's unfailing love like it.

Many years ago our college friends said they voted us the couple least likely to succeed. Tragically, many of the marriages of the far more suitable couples we knew have disintegrated, but the stubborn love of Jesus Christ kept us hanging on. Had Keith and I remained those two people who walked the aisle together, we would simply be another statistic. He and I often laugh about the pleadings of one of his groomsmen the day we married. "Keith, I really hope you won't let marriage change you." *Oh, brother.* Through the years God has tended us, broken us, and mended us until we've found ourselves married to people hardly resembling the ones we met at the altar twenty-something years ago. We are convinced that all we did then was fall in love with the faintest glimpse of who God was going to make us. He is *still* making us.

As Keith and I contemplated the seriousness of marriage, we realized that it was the "until death do you part" clause that unsettled us. In order to make a lifetime prospect a little more bearable, we decided before we married that we were simply signing a fifty-year lease with an option to renew. During the ceremony we smiled at each other when the pastor read the clause, and we replaced it mentally with our own. We've never forgotten our deal. When we get into a fuss, one of us invariably will say, "OK. That's it. I'm not going to renew my lease." It rarely fails to bring a grin to a grinless moment. When one of us does something really thoughtful, the other commonly says, "That renewal option is really looking good right about now." Strangely, when we married, a lifetime seemed far too long. Now, as the years pass so quickly and we realize we won't be married in heaven, a lifetime doesn't seem long enough. The thought of our inevitable earthly good-bye brings tears to us both.

Keith and I have not had a marriage without regrets. But we do not regret our marriage. Keith is a very reserved man, yet he loves me unreservedly. He is a man not many people really know. *I* know him. That makes *me* special. I am a passionate woman. I am passionate about Christ. I am passionate about His precepts. I am passionate about His church. And I have passion in my heart that God has approved and appointed for Keith alone. That makes *him* special. I'll still see him from a distance at times and think, *That good-lookin' man is mine.* Often he'll take a seat and wait in the back of my Sunday school class for his long-winded wife to finish her lesson. His face becomes one of many . . . but it is the only one that looks at me with the affection of a man toward his wife. We are each other's in a way that no one else can have us. A singular gift of God. We laugh together until we cry. We cry together until we laugh. We have slow danced a million miles on the linoleum while supper boiled over on the stove.

We are a miracle. Until death does us part or our fifty-year lease expires, I'll remember the day I realized just what a miracle we were. Melissa and several of her friends were in her room listening to a country-western station on the radio, talking a hundred miles an hour. I was directly downstairs in the kitchen eavesdropping not only on every word *they* were saying, but every word they were listening to. I had raised them on contemporary Christian music, and I was just beginning to let them test their wings with the smallest tastes of some other kinds of music. All of a sudden, a song came on the radio and Melissa blurted out, "Everybody be quiet! I love this song!" I strained with interest to hear the nature of the song my child "loved." As all the jabbering ceased, I heard her say, "This song reminds me of . . ." I was nearly slain by her next words: ". . . *my* parents." It was a love song. I stood in the kitchen and cried. *Thank You, God. Thank You.*

Both of our children have said they want a marriage like ours. *That* is a miracle. Keith and I are taken aback by the pure grace of God to redeem what seemed at times unredeemable. We are a testimony that God is more powerful than our pasts. Mightier than our differences. And far more stubborn than we are. If God graciously allows us to live out our "lease" and grow old together, we will undoubtedly have challenges ahead. How I pray we have developed a love that can no longer be killed . . . but if perchance we haven't, Christ's eternal voice still shouts, "Lazarus, come forth!" May our hearts bear the marks of resurrection.

Those twelve roses brought to our front door several years ago are still in our daughter's room—dried, with faded ribbon intact. Not because she pines for something past but because she waits for something future. Our girls were not taught to believe in fairy tales. Keith and I had no such luxury. They were taught to believe in *romance.* Even the resurrection kind. May they echo the laughter of God with their life partner and dance their shiny linoleum dull while dinner boils over and their skeptics are proved wrong. Love is worth living.

Melissa didn't always
need a hairbrush.

Coiffing while we still could . . .
her hair was on its way.

CHAPTER 8

THE STRING ON THE DRAWER KNOB

Poor Keith. The man appears to have been destined for a household of women. He grew up as the only brother to three sisters and ended up with a wife, two daughters, and three female canines. He deliberately brought home a "male" cat just to make a point. That "point" proceeded to have a litter of kittens the next spring. The challenge of being surrounded by females has not been easy for a "man's man" of Keith's sort. He is forever stepping on our tender toes with his foot-long cowboy boots. When will men ever learn that when we ask for their opinions, rarely do we really want them? Most of the time, what we want is their affirmation—even if they have to stretch the truth a tad to give it. Isn't that what *marriage license* means?

As far as Keith is concerned, the girls speak in other tongues. I often take it upon myself to exercise a self-appointed gift of interpretation. "Honey, I know that's what she *said*, but that's not what she *meant*." Actually, the man is a veritable saint about this posse of women. Those same cowboy boots that step on our toes at times also follow us all over the mall, stand outside untold dressing rooms, then walk to the counter where Keith surrenders his wallet from the back pocket of his Wranglers. A good man indeed.

Surely God has a special reward for men who are the lone rangers on a ranch full of females. Perhaps the place He's preparing for them has a big screen television that gets only *ESPN,* a bottomless bag of Fritos, and an endless supply of bean dip. A place where they can kick off their boots and their socks don't smell. Now, that's living. Then again, if there's only one channel, what use is remote control? Can it really be heaven without remote control? I suppose we'll have to leave that to God. Only He knows what compensation He has for men who have served a life sentence in Girl World. Perhaps it will be enough never to hear the word *hormones* again. Keith has had to discuss all sorts of things he didn't even care to know existed. He gets that contorted look on his face like he's in excruciating pain and says, "Not that again!" Yes, *that.*

Oh, he does love his girls, though. To me, home is where our house is. To Keith, home is where his girls are. That house means nothing to him without us in it. If we're not home, he does everything he can to avoid it. Of course, there are certain times when we're home that he deems best to avoid being there. Like when we're going to watch *Steel Magnolias* for the twenty-seventh time. Or when we drag all our manicure and pedicure paraphernalia out into the family room. Keith has made the best of it though. He's even discovered that a little touch of fluorescent nail polish on some of his lures really attracts the fish. Where would he be without us?

Just for the record, Keith is not the only one who has made sacrifices because he has daughters. After all, does he ever storm out of his closet demanding to know who borrowed his basic black skirt? The girls and I have had the mixed blessing of being able to wear many of the same size clothes. Convenient at times; a nightmare at others. Oddly, since the second one also went off to college, I am losing touch with what a nightmare it could be. A few weeks after Melissa moved into the dorm, I started to cry. Keith looked at me compassionately and said, "Are you missing your daughters again?" I blurted out, "No. Right this minute I'm missing their *clothes.*"

Missing clothes have not been the biggest bone of contention in our version of Girl World, however. Missing *brushes* have. Maybe it's just me, but I have a hard time rolling and styling my hair without a brush. Only He who counts the stars can count the times I have been stranded brushless. The scenario was identical almost every time. I would kiss the girls good-bye as they headed to kindergarten or middle school or high school. I'd walk back in the house, jump in the shower, wash my hair, open the bathroom drawer, and *poof!* Another brush had magically disappeared. If you don't curse *then,* you know you don't curse. That has been my solitary consolation.

The girls would like to have convinced me that the brushes had gone to be with Jesus, but I knew better. The brushes had gone to be with *them.* Right about now, my eldest is pleading innocence. In all fairness she was not the one with the hairbrush stronghold. She probably only swiped a few dozen. My youngest, on the other hand, needed a support group to give it up. Until then, what she really needed was a bigger locker. I am quite certain that every time she opened her locker, at least sixty-three hairbrushes spilled out onto the floor. I can also picture a dozen seventeen-year-old valley girls standing around while the ceiling rained hairbrushes, flicking their long, straight manes to the other side and saying, *"Cool,"* . . . with at least two syllables.

I tried everything. I got all of us our own personal hairbrushes and wrote our names on them with magic marker. Not the least deterrent. *Keith-brush, Beth-brush, Amanda-brush,* and *Melissa-brush* all hopped the nearest school bus and bounced in record time right into the locker. It's not like the child was unaware. She knew exactly what she was doing. She simply felt that if we were decent parents, we'd understand it was essential that she have a hairbrush on her way to school. She had simply left hers there the day before. *Hers?* And we really didn't expect her to drive to school without one . . . *did* we? Furthermore, why did I care so much, she once asked me? After all, "You've already caught *your* man." Yes, and if it's all the same to you, I'd like to keep him.

One day the perfect solution hit me. It came in a moment of inspiration while I was complaining that I couldn't seem to keep up with anything that wasn't "tied down." "That's it! I'll tie them down!" I made a beeline to the grocery store and snapped up two hairbrushes that had holes at the base of the handles. With a satisfied smirk upon my face, I took two ample pieces of household string and tied one hairbrush to my bathroom drawer and another to Keith's. It was nothing less than a stroke of genius. And it worked. For days we each had a hairbrush. Never mind that the two-foot string didn't leave much room for teasing the back of my hair. And Keith didn't seem to mind bending over to brush his hair. It was a small price to pay. We discussed the brilliance of the plan every single morning while getting ready. Not only was it good for my hair, it was good for my ego. I had taken control of the situation. Clearly, I pulled some weight around that house. Ah, yes. Those were some of the best weeks of our lives.

Then it happened.

First it was Keith's. I appreciate that the culprit (who remains unnamed) took into consideration that the man of the house had less hair to coif. It is a well-raised child who knows to choose the lesser of two evils. After all, my brush was still tied down securely. For about a week. Then . . .

There they were. Two foot-long strings dangling uselessly from the drawer knobs. *Mocking me.* No one ever confessed to the crime. The weapon, a pair of scissors with bright green handles, was found at the crime scene. I considered just cutting my hair to the scalp with them, but I knew that was the martyr complex in me. I decided to snatch the chief suspect bald-headed instead. Tying the brushes to the drawer knob was a good idea. I just know it was. I never tried it again, however. I couldn't take it. With the few inches of string left behind, Keith and I would have had to put our faces in the drawer to brush our hair. We did what many other parents have done, but few have admitted. We surrendered. Why? Because that's just about the worst thing the child has done. *So far.* She, like her sister, is an exquisite creature who makes me laugh until I cry and knows when to take me seriously . . . but she is serious about not letting *me* know it.

I have learned that there are some things in life you just can't tie down. Children are one of them. Incidentally, I never cut that string off my bathroom drawer knob. I just trimmed it a tad. It serves as a wonderful reminder that some things were never meant to be tied down. Ever since I've looked at life from an empty nest, the words of the familiar proverb have taken on a different inflection. "Train a child in the way he *should go,* and when he is old he will not turn from it" (Prov. 22:6, emphasis mine). I have been reminded that we train up our children precisely so they can *go.* That's how it *should* be. A very wise woman said to me, "Look at it this way, Beth. Their going is better than their staying." I'll take her word for it. Another friend said, "Be careful what you wish. Lots of young adults are like boomerangs. You keep trying to throw them out on their own, and they just keep landing back in your yard." The fact is, too many adults in one household can tend to be . . . let's see, how should we put this . . . too many.

I've accepted to some degree that I may not be able to tie down my children, but I firmly believe that we should try like mad to tie down what we can. I learned through some difficult times that you'd better have a few things tied down—things that you *know that you know*—so you can get through the things you don't. Some things in life I know for a fact. Things that a head-on collision of my circumstances and God's Word have proven to me beyond a doubt . . . like God knows us intimately and loves us completely and that He is for us and not against us. I no longer believe these things by *faith.* I know them as *fact.* Other things aren't quite so clear. Situations in which we can't accurately use words like *always* and *never.* In this colorful life we live, where sometimes we'd prefer black and white, faith often comes in the shade of gray. Things not so easily proven. Not so easily tied down. Goodness knows I've tried, but someone keeps getting that same pair of scissors with the bright green handles and cutting my carefully tied strings.

In my lifelong search for something tangible I could hold onto . . . something that I, like a two-year-old child, could call *mine,* I found a whole treasury. Above all, God's words can be tied down. In fact, He suggests we do exactly that. "Fix these words of mine in your hearts and minds; tie them as symbols on your hands and bind them on your foreheads" (Deut. 11:18). Deuteronomy 29:29 says, "The secret things belong to the LORD our God, but the things revealed belong to us and to our children forever." I love the word *forever.* That word will tie down every time.

By the way, Melissa ended up having the last say on the hairbrushes. The morning after I got home from taking her to college, I was trying my hardest to look on the bright side. I muttered, "Just think, Beth, about all you *don't* have to do this morning." I jumped in the shower, washed my hair, then I opened the bathroom drawer and *poof!* The brush had magically disappeared. *One last time.* I laughed my head off. I don't know if Deuteronomy 11:18 applies loosely to a hairbrush, but perhaps if I had bound it to my forehead, I could have hung onto it. It would have been convenient. It might not have stopped her, but I would've seen those scissors coming.

These days I always find my hairbrush right where I left it. But the knob I use to open the drawer has a very conspicuous string dangling from it . . . reminding me what *is* missing. I'd give up all the brushes in the world *and* my basic black skirt just to have her back. But some things you just can't tie down.

Amanda at four. Who cares about being a
flower girl when there are pictures to
color and scenes to create?

I've always thought this picture captured
my little dreamer. Amanda still has a way
of seeing things out a window that
no one else seems to see.

CHAPTER 9

DOROTHY'S RED SHOES

I was raised on Walt Disney movies and Rodgers and Hammerstein musicals. After retiring from the military, my dad ran the local "picture show" in our small Arkansas town. As inconceivable as this may be to a thirty-something or younger, our movie house was a one-screener. We usually ran the same movie for two or three weeks, plenty of time for a few good breezes to blow away several of the letters of the title off the marquee. It was just as well. Dad was feeling sorry for a young man who desperately needed a job, and so he hired him to hang the letters. He was as good a man with a ladder as I have ever seen but, with all due respect, spelling wasn't his strong suit. The old cowboy classic *Shane* was *Shame.* The suave and debonair James Bond swept audiences off their feet as Agent 007 in *Goldfinker.* We won't even discuss the disgrace that befell *Mary Poppins.*

Now that I think of it, the majority of Dad's employees weren't much better. With few exceptions they were *us.* And by that I mean my brothers and sisters and me. In retrospect it occurs to me that my daddy was no dummy. We weren't much help, but we were cheap. Pocket change and glad to get it. I served popcorn and Coke when folks could get them both for a quarter. I was no older than seven when I stood on my highest tiptoes to put the cup to the fountain drink lever. The only way I knew it was full was when it ran over. My younger brother did the same thing. Hence, the floor stayed pretty sticky. A Green (my maiden name) kid could be identified by the way our shoes stuck to the floor when we walked. *Coke syrup.* We did our best to avoid shag carpet.

Still, we were the best show in town. Located smack dab in the center of Main Street, we were right across the street from Fuller Drug Store and just a block or so from the Piggly Wiggly. Everybody who was anybody came to the movie because in those days there wasn't much everybody wasn't willing to see. It was a wonderful way to grow up. Like practically everyone else, my young life was a mixed bag of all sorts of things, good and bad. Great and horrible. But when "break time" came, I could slip out of the concession stand and sit right down on the back row of the tiny auditorium and get lost in a movie. Dad wouldn't let us use the real soft drink cups and the popcorn buckets, but we could drink to our heart's content out of a Dixie cup and eat a whole pickle bag full of popcorn. It was hog heaven.

I saw most of the movies so many times that I knew every word. I can still sing every song in *The Sound of Music* by heart. Too bad no one wants me to. I also saw a few movies I had no business seeing, but for the most part, I soaked in themes of "love conquers all" and "happily ever after." I can remember like yesterday the first movie I ever saw that broke the rules. Somebody should have been watching while I was slipping into *Romeo and Juliet.* Not only was it far too mature for me, it disturbed me terribly. If we didn't have "happily ever after," what on earth did we have? Who in the world wants to see a movie with an unhappy ending? I'd much rather a movie lie to me than stab me with an unhappy reality. If I want reality, I'll stay home, watch the news, and have it for free. Give me a feel-good movie, or save your celluloid. Doris Day and Rock Hudson. Now those were people you could trust with your moviegoing back in those days.

Even back then, some movies just weren't worth seeing. On the other hand, some were timeless classics. *The Wizard of Oz* was one of those. I don't remember how long it played at our one-screen theater, but I assure you I only saw it once in my childhood. It scared the ever-lovin' daylights out of me. We heard a good deal about "hell" growing up in a Baptist church, and about the worst place I could imagine was something like the ghastly castle of the "wicked witch of the West." Those flying monkeys still give me the creeps. Call me the Cowardly Lion, but I'd just as soon stay out of a storm in Kansas. And that Wizard. Was he a disappointment, or what? My worst fear was that God would turn out like him. *He didn't.*

In so many ways my firstborn has been a cookie cutter of her mother. Although she has far more of her father's reserve, she has her momma's heart. She so desperately wanted to believe that life was a Walt Disney movie and that everybody lives happily ever after. She much preferred to be shielded from any of the world's unpleasantries . . . probably because her mom tried so hard to help her believe there weren't any.

I knew better but felt strongly that there was no sense in *her* knowing any better. I figured that if I raised her right, she'd never have to know. *Wrong.* But I'll come back to that later.

Growing up, Amanda loved movies almost as much as I did. Her grandfather still ran the local picture show when she was a little girl, but by this time, he had moved to the Texas multiscreen. We picked and chose our flicks carefully, so Amanda usually watched just what I wanted her to watch. Dreamy movies about dreamy lives. She was a dreamer at heart with an imagination that could challenge Steven Spielberg. To me, the only thing better than a movie was sitting back and watching her play, listening to her imagine. She could turn the den into a movie set with adorable genius. One of the nicest things I could possibly say about her display of imagination is that she made me want a pickle bag of popcorn and a Dixie cup of Coca-Cola.

We held on to imaginary worlds of happily ever after for as long as we could, but as she grew, so did her world. Her first brush with reality, however, didn't come from the world. It came from her mother's own womb . . . in the form of a little sister whose life calling appeared to be shattering Amanda's loftier notions. *With joyful abandon,* I might add. Most of what Amanda created with her Play-Doh, Melissa ate. Every fairy tale scene Amanda built in our den, Melissa drove through with her Big Wheel. As soon as the little dickens could hold a pair of blunt children's scissors in her hand, she cut all the manes off Amanda's Pretty Ponies. I cannot count the times Amanda cried, "Mommy, Melissa won't play right!" I just hate it when people don't play right, don't you? I happen to think every healthy kid has a right to make-believe, so sometimes I entered the scene with a wooden spoon, and the show-stealer got paddled off the stage. If Melissa's dramatic exit brought Amanda to a standing ovation, I threatened her with it too. Brother! Trying to keep a fairy tale in the home is hard work!

Amanda is a grown young woman now. She figured out that unfortunately life is not a Disney movie and that sometimes opposites attract more fire than fireworks. I knew she was developing into a tad more of a realist the first time I took her on an overseas trip. An interesting topic of conversation came up between a number of us on the excursion: "If you could give the world anything besides Jesus, what would it be?" Amanda, seventeen at the time, chimed in uncharacteristically and with deep insight: "Deodorant." *Amen*. Parts of life simply do not smell good. That's all there is to it. Some are unavoidable. Some have had the gall to waft through our house. But the occasional stench of reality has not been able to steal something very precious—and almost indefinable—from her sweet soul. In many respects she's still a dreamer who believes life—and people—can be better than you think. If she could, she'd focus only on experiences that show her that real life can be just as good, just as noble, and just as happy as fiction.

Her room still bears signs of fictional movie life. Not just any movie. *The Wizard of Oz*. A music box, a snow globe, a cookie jar, posters, figurines, and a bed-size blanket all remind us of an imaginary adventure between a girl, her dog, a tin man, a lion, and a scarecrow. The centerpiece is a replica of Dorothy's glittery red shoes sitting on a white shelf. The theme for Amanda's room was my idea as much as hers.

When she was a little girl, she had a recurring nightmare that she was caught in a tornado. Maybe our choice for her room was a gentle reminder that folks really can survive seasons in their lives when harsh winds come twisting and destroying—and not only in the movies.

I wanted so badly to be the perfect mother and raise my children in the perfect home. Not that I had ever had it or ever seen it. The irony is that as hard as I worked to keep harsh realities out of their lives, my children learned a few right inside our own home. Let's face it. No family lives a fairy tale. Rich or poor, saved or lost—life is hard. Ours was no exception. Keith and I were at a loss to shield our children from the difficulties of life. For heaven's sake, someone would have had to shield our children from *us*. We each had plenty of our own difficulties. We were not the healthiest two souls that ever became "one." We were more like two speeding vehicles that had a head-on collision no wrecker could pull apart. Thank goodness.

Blessed resiliency! I am convinced that a family that pays half a wit to a powerful and merciful God has faith enough to be far stronger than it thinks. We're absolute proof of that. As it turns out, our girls didn't get a chance to delude themselves into thinking only "other" homes have problems. We had plenty of challenges, some of which were tremendously serious, yet God has enabled us to walk, crawl, limp, or leap—whatever way we could progress—toward wholeness. We have lived family life in a perpetual course of overcoming. One thing behind us, another thing in front of us. As God would have it, the more we had behind us, the less we feared what was ahead of us.

I am so grateful for the mercy of God that rained on our roof. God reminds me at times not only to be thankful for the things that have happened but for the things that have *not*. Neither of our daughters appears to struggle with resentment nor a lack of respect for their parents even though we, like a host of other parents, made plenty of mistakes. Perhaps even more interestingly, neither child has shown a single sign of resenting a parent (a mother at that!) immersed in ministry. So many do. I have no words to describe my gratitude that ours don't.

I believe there are two primary reasons the girls aren't resentful after so many challenges. The foremost is the absolute grace and mercy of a *huge* God who was simply bigger than our challenges. To every Christian home, please allow me to say that God is *for* you, not against you. The "lot" He does with a cooperative "little" exceeds the astonishing. The second reason is also a grace gift of God. It was not one I could have really seen for myself. It's something I realized was part of our home from overhearing my children speak of it through the years. Melissa implied it recently as she prayed before a large group I was about to address. "Lord, we don't want anybody to get the idea our family is perfect. It's *not*. But I thank You, God, that because of You, it's *real*."

I'm not sure anything outweighs the importance of authenticity in the home, particularly to young people who are raised in a churchgoing or Christian home. The impact of authenticity *or inauthenticity* is mammoth. Teenagers, for all sorts of reasons, may not be the best at *living* what is real, but they are quite adept at *judging* what is real. Particularly from the front-row seat of their own homes. As many parents know, they are often willing to call Mom or Dad's hand at the least infraction . . . if they have the freedom, that is. Some are raised in such harsh and dictatorial homes that the children wouldn't dare say a word, but they still recognize insincerity. Seeing one kind of parent at home and another kind of person in public, particularly at church, can cause the child anything from lack of respect to a lifelong and nearly incapacitating root of bitterness. How I thank God for the many genuine—albeit imperfect—servants of God out there! Perhaps I'm naïve, but I truly believe they are the majority. At the same time, if I could count the occasions adults have come to me embittered or hindered by childhood homes of Christian hypocrisy, the numbers would be staggering.

I'm not sure teens have the least expectation for their parents to be perfect, but they do indeed demand that they be real . . . *or else*. (And you can bet there will be an "else" of one kind or another, even if the parents remain unaware.) Insincerity and gross inconsistency undoubtedly have repercussions. When we're wrong, they want us to take responsibility and ask for forgiveness. No, not grovel. We are the parents and they are the children, and the last thing we need is a role reversal. But if we don't take responsibility for not practicing what we preach, how in the world will our children learn consistency? Our children want us to mean what we say and follow through on our promises. They have respect for parents who take responsibility for wrong decisions or wrong habits then work diligently to change them. Children all the way through their teens and young adult years really are amazingly forgiving. They are even surprisingly patient when we take two steps forward and one step back if they see sincerity and progress.

I know a Christian family that was nearly torn to shreds by the alcoholism of one parent and the equally harmful enabling of the other. The masks went on every Sunday as they got out of their car at church and came off soon after they returned home. Church was a Disney movie and home was a horror film. The children loved their parents, but they were terribly hurt by their decisions, confused by their duplicity, and had virtually no respect for them. Then, something amazing happened. After a terrible crisis, the parents took responsibility for their actions, asked forgiveness, and promised to do whatever they had to do for their home to be healthy. The road was long and grueling, but, to the glory of God, the family made it. The children are adults now and have nothing but love and respect for their parents because they watched them work *hard* to overcome. Today the couple is the same whether at church or at home. So are their grown children. Their parents weren't perfect, but the children had the privilege of watching them become healthy and real.

A friend of mine, whose pet peeve is insincerity, often says to the church, "For heaven's sake, *be what you seem.*" Whether in a youth group or in a private home, most young people see no difference whatsoever between glimpses of insincerity and outright hypocrisy. They want us to be what we seem. Actually, so does God. Christ never resisted the heinous, habitual sinner who was desperate to repent, but He could not abide a religious hypocrite. The New Testament usage of the term *hypocrisy* came from its application in Greek drama. "In the Greek theater, a hypocrite was one who wore a mask and played a part on the stage, imitating the speech, mannerisms, and conduct of the character portrayed" (*Nelson's New Illustrated Bible Dictionary,* p. 587).

Like Amanda, all young people love movies; they just want the actors to stay on the screen and out of the home. Our children are looking for nonfiction families. The real thing. People whose spiritual walks match their spiritual talk. They don't need their parents to be perfect, but they prefer that their parents don't pretend. They just want us to be real. If we're not the real thing, what's to keep young people from fearing that God may not be the real thing either? Inauthenticity among people of the faith makes the youth of that generation fear that God may turn out to be something like the wizard of Oz.

I can still picture Dorothy's face when she and her friends realized that "the wonderful wizard" they'd been told to seek was really no wizard at all. She had placed all her hopes in nothing but a hoax. As young as I was, I can remember feeling almost sick inside when Dorothy looked behind the curtain and saw that she had cast her hopes on someone just as weak and mortal as she. My strong emotional reaction had very little to do with an imaginary story line about a girl who went from the eye of a tornado to the Land of Oz. I knew the movie was make-believe. But what's not make-believe is the devastation that can result from being "made to believe" a lie, especially one that concerns our heroes. I think deep down inside all of us, we are absolutely terrified of placing our hopes and dreams in something that we'll discover is not even real. Masses of people out there are scared to death that God may be little more than the wizard of Oz. All volume and no action. That Jesus was a good man. A prophet perhaps, but the Son of God? Couldn't it all just be make-believe? You and I know better. The God behind this curtain is real, huge, and omnipotent. Far beyond our wildest imaginations. If the veil were drawn back while we were still mortals, we wouldn't survive the shock of His greatness. He has left us here to bear witness to what we know of Him. We were never called to explain God. We were called to be witnesses of what we've seen and experienced of Him. Nothing is more powerful or harder to refute than simple testimonies like "I was lost but now am found." "I was blind but now I see." "I was bound but now I'm free." "I was lame but now I walk." In other words, "I am changed and only a living and powerful God could have changed me." Few things have the impact of authentically transformed lives—real victors who are living, breathing proof of a very real God.

Authenticity is as critical for parents inside their home as it is for pastors inside their church. Whether we signed up for the responsibility or not, Christian parents give their children impressions of what they can expect from God. Our trustworthiness implies His trustworthiness. How desperately our younger generation longs for the redeemed of the Lord not only to "say so" but to "live so" and be what we seem.

Now, here's hope for the hopeless. Every word of this has just come from a former hypocrite. Yep, for much of my young life and just enough of my adult life to propel me to authentic living for the rest of my days. I didn't mean to be one. I'm not sure I thought I had a choice. I knew enough to know that God is real and that the godly life was truly attainable, but after constant tries and failures, I was convinced it was out of *my* reach. I was so desperate to "be" godly; yet I had such a handicapped soul, the closest I ever got to "being" was "acting," hoping my heart would one day catch up with my act. I was a fairly vocal Christian who believed the things I was saying with all my heart. I just felt powerless to live them out consistently. The way I saw it, living it some of the time was better than none of the time. Sadly, the result was that I disintegrated my witness to those who knew better than to believe I was who I seemed. I could have started a "Hypocrites Anonymous" support group . . . except that hypocrites aren't nearly as anonymous as they'd like to think. God has mercifully given me the opportunity to ask forgiveness from those I felt I confused or misled. I desperately needed them to know that Christ was real even when I wasn't.

How I praise God for His loving-kindness! For His endless patience to take me by the hand and teach me how to stumble without always falling. For His healing Word that created in me a purer heart, healthy enough to live what I believed with some level of consistency. My children have not seen perfection by a long shot. But, to the grace of God, neither have they seen hypocrisy. I finally left the act to the movies. Recently in an interview I was asked what one thing in ministry has meant more to me in a personal realm than any other. The answer came to me immediately: *That my children choose to come to my classes.* It is my practice to kneel before a group and pray before I speak or teach. I can't tell you what it has meant to me to kneel countless times at the feet of my own two daughters who often sat right there on the front row. *Merciful Savior, how good You are.*

So there. Amanda's not Dorothy. I'm not Auntie Em. Our home isn't Kansas. And our God certainly isn't the wizard of Oz. But I'd like to think that no matter how big her world gets—red shoes or no red shoes—she might just click her heels together occasionally, smile, and say, "There's no place like home."

Life on the other side of the fence
seemed so far removed back then.
Now they've jumped the fence and run.

What's so wonderful about being little
is that we still have the ability to
hear the songs the wildflowers sing.

$\mathcal{T}$HE SONGS

Considering there's not a single singer in our bunch, we've sung more songs than the family Von Trapp. That we are not traveling in a broken-down bus from country church to country church certainly isn't from lack of practice. We sing our hearts out for the pure enjoyment of it. What a joyous gift God gave us when He gave us song! If I could only get a song out of my mouth the way it sounds in my soul, I'd be beside myself!

I wonder whether music is something created or if it is something eternal. Something that existed between the Father, Son, and Holy Spirit before God ever said, "Let there be . . ." Can you imagine the Trinity in three-part harmony? There again, perhaps the Three-in-One were so in tune with one another, they all sang melody. Where did "song" origi-nate? Did David, the psalmist and the "man after God's own heart," discover his songs right there . . . *in God's own heart?* If so, would this mean his songs were eternal? Could the harp be earth's way of whispering the sounds of heaven's breezes? Is the piano an echo of the happy river of God? Doesn't Scripture say that some heavenly voices are like the sound of a trumpet? The answers are beyond me but not the questions.

One thing we can know for sure: music existed long before we did. When "the LORD answered Job out of the storm," He said:

> "Where were you when I laid the earth's foundation?
>   Tell me, if you understand.
> Who marked off its dimensions? Surely you know!
>   Who stretched a measuring line across it?
> On what were its footings set,
>   or who laid its cornerstone—
> while the morning stars *sang together*
>   and all the angels shouted for joy?"
>
> (Job 38:1, 4–7, emphasis mine)

Imagine the angels singing glorious hallelujahs as God called the world into existence! Picture the universal fireworks of millions of stars bursting into the skies. Maybe that's when music was born. Perhaps it was compulsory. Unwritten, unrehearsed, unrestrained! Adoration demanding a higher language than simple, spoken words. Some things were never meant to be said. They were meant to be sung.

I can't wait to hear the songs of heaven. I wonder if they will be altogether different than ours or if the noblest composers simply listened closely enough to "hear" something that cannot be heard . . . save with spiritual ears. A celestial score written on a terrestrial scale. And somehow we sense it. Songs that move us—make us tremble—make us stand—make us bow—or make us cry. And we don't know why. We call them *inspired*. Maybe they are instead *transpired*. I wonder when a fitful people, so given to selfishness and division, finally unify as one voice in glorious praise . . . if we are suddenly singing along with the heavenly hosts? Or do they celebrate the rare moment and sing along with us?

Oh, the gift of song! From lamentations to thankful adorations, no season is without a song if we can bear to sing it. Job 35:9–10 muses:

> Men cry out under a load of oppression;
> > they plead for relief from the arm of the powerful.
> But no one says, "Where is God my Maker,
> > who gives songs in the night."

I believe the verse is suggesting that while we groan under our load, we can pray for far more than relief. We can ask the Lord our Maker for a song in our night. We can emerge from any season of life with a new stanza for the old chorus: "This is my story! This is my song!" Surely that's what David meant when he wrote:

> I waited patiently for the Lord;
> > he turned to me and heard my cry.
> He lifted me out of the slimy pit,
> > out of the mud and mire;
> he set my feet on a rock
> > and gave me a firm place to stand.
> He put a new song in my mouth,
> > a hymn of praise to our God.

(Ps. 40:1–3)

Many new songs come out of hard places. Masterpieces are not written in mediocrity.

I love music. I never live a day without it. I sing with it. I dance with it. And I lift up my joyful noise to God as an offering of the heart—if a sacrifice to the ear. I've tried hard not to let my children live a day without it either. We started nice and early. After all the physiological problems I had inherited from my mother, I was scared to death I would not be able to have children. I was told I would need surgery to correct the problem. Dr. God must have performed it without my knowledge. All I know is that two months after I married, I was throwing up in the morning, absolutely certain I was allergic to marriage. Thankfully, no such luck. Our firstborn was on her way and I was ecstatic.

I had a rocking chair in our extra bedroom practically by the time the circle had formed on the bottom of the test tube. I don't know if lullabies were created for babies or if babies were created for lullabies. I just know they go together. I rocked and sang to that precious child long before I traded my blue jeans for maternity pants. I sang every hymn I could think of. (I had to leave out the third verse on almost all of them. Our church only sang verses one, two, and four. I always felt sorry for verse three. They're all recorded in some hymnbook in heaven. I just know it.) I also sang more traditional lullabies, but I didn't know many of them. "Rock-a-bye Baby" was out of the question. Who in the world would rock her baby from a treetop? And, furthermore, who wants to sing, "And down will come baby, cradle and all"? Who wrote that song, for heaven's sake? And where was Child Protective Services?

Finally, I no longer had to sing to a child I couldn't see. I had a babe in arms. I was so taken with motherhood, I never laid my first child down in her bed for her nap. I rocked her for two to three hours every afternoon. Did I need a job, or what? In the course of that many hours, a soul can either turn on the soap operas, which I did aplenty in those days, or go through a wide repertoire of songs. That's when I learned that one has to be careful about what one sings. And, even then, one has to be careful about what one's child *thinks* one sang. OK. Maybe "Amazing Grace" was not the best song to sing while rocking a child. There I was, singing to my child about what a "wretch" her mother was. That was something for me to know and her to find out! I should have stuck with "Silent Night." I certainly was longing for one. I'll never forget hearing Amanda belt out with the words to "Amazing Grace" one day when she was three years old. With sizzling passion she burst, "Amazing gwace, how sweet the sound that saved a gwouch like me!" She didn't know what a wretch was, but I assure you, she occasionally knew what a grouch was.

When Amanda was old enough to start singing with me, I knew it was time for her to lie down in a bed for her afternoon nap. Especially when she started correcting me on the words. It was just as well. Melissa was on the way by that time. Trying to rock a two-year-old while great with child is a challenge many of us moms have experienced. What precious memories, though! I would sing, Amanda would squirm, and Melissa would kick. "That silly baby is kicking me again, Mommy!" "That's because she wants to play with you, honey." That's what *I* thought. Through the years, she kicked Amanda a whole lot more than she played sweetly with her. Cantankerous little dickens. Thankfully, now Amanda gets a kick out of her sister in a nicer way. Amanda deserves some kind of medal. A Purple Heart or something. They fought almost every waking moment *unless* we were singing . . . which may explain my vain attempts to make our lives an opera.

Singing was almost a no-fail prescription for peace on a road trip. Living in Houston means you never go anywhere quickly. Even going to the grocery store was a half-day adventure. Our church was fourteen miles from our house, and my parents lived just short of two hours from our front door. The Moores definitely had quality car time. We had every kids' praise tape known to man. We had Scripture memory tapes with catchy tunes. You name it, we sang it. But as much as my children liked the prewritten lyrics of professionals, they often preferred the songs I made up. That's right. I made them up. Usually as I went along. And yes, of course, they were embarrassingly silly, but what kid doesn't love silly?

Actually, I inherited the "gift." My mom used to do the same thing. She would make up a song about whatever baby she happened to be rocking, and it would go on for half an eternity until she or the baby fell asleep. In case you're thinking, "What a talented woman!"—*don't*. My mother didn't sing any better than I do. The lyrics never rhymed nor even stayed with the same tune. They weren't pretty. Half the time they didn't even make sense. But just like most of the things our parents do, we do the same things anyway. And may I say these songs were a hit? The reason my children loved them so much is because the homemade songs were always about *them*. Personalized. And about the most random subjects you can imagine. It was easy, really. I'd just start singing about the child, using her name a lot, and would chime on about whatever came to mind. Let me see if I can work up a prime example. One might have gone something like this:

> Amanda is a sweetie girl
> She has a dog named Coney
> She runs the fastest of her friends
> Because Amanda has new shoes
> That she's learning how to tie
> Because she is so smart
> And Amanda has a ponytail
> And she likes ketchup on her French fries. . . .

And so on and so on and so on. Get the picture? Now put those words to notes that don't blend, change the entire tune every two or three lines, and picture the child trying to sing along at the top of her lungs, and you've got it. This was not what you'd catalog under "inspirational." You couldn't have sworn it by my children, however. From the time they could talk, they would say, "Please sing a song about *me*, Mommy!" What child is not her very favorite subject matter? In my young days I was far too sanctimonious to mix our sillier songs with our spiritual songs, but nap time was a prime time for the *me songs*. I would simply get quieter and quieter until that particular "me" was sound asleep in my arms, looking like an angel. My last line was almost always the same: "Then she fell fast asleep." And it was worth it.

Our personal brand of sing-song had its downside. On too many occasions, one of the girls would say, "Not *that* song about me, Mommy. The *other* song!" I would respond, "*What* other song, honey?" The answer was the same every time: "The one you sang *yesterday.*" Any mother knows that "yesterday" to a preschooler is any time before that very second. Needless to say, I couldn't remember for the life of me what I had sung the last time. If the child was in a fretful mood, my inability to produce the former lyric and tune brought about no small displeasure. Don't think I don't know what rock stars go through. The pressure to perform as well as you did last time is unbearable.

The worst fallout we had from our singing habits came unexpectedly at request time when the children were old enough to be in preschool and kindergarten. The music teacher would make the tragic mistake of asking for requests of the children's favorite songs. You guessed it. My children invariably requested one from our homemade variety. They were so annoyed when their music teacher didn't know the song.

"She doesn't know *anything.*"

I would say sheepishly, "Then don't even bother to ask her for one again. Just request something *plain.*" Translation: *normal.* Later, when they realized *why* her repertoire was so sadly lacking, they nearly killed me. They blamed me. I blamed my mother.

Michael took his time adopting some of our Moore-isms, but he caught on to the sing-songs in a heartbeat. He was a very tiny four when he first came to live with us. His stature looked far more like that of a two-and-a-half-year-old.

To my knowledge and by his early admissions, he had never been rocked and sung to before. We quickly started making up for lost time. Oh, how he loved it! He would often squeal like we were riding a roller coaster. I can't think of a single time when rocking ever put Michael to sleep. No, indeed. He wouldn't have dared miss a moment of it. He sat straight up in my lap with eyes as big as saucers, spitting out the next song request before I could finish the other. "Faster, Mommy. Faster!" We put a million miles on that old chair. I'll never forget once being told that I babied him too much. Perhaps I did. But some folks could use a little extra babying. I have regrets, but those times are not among them.

I learned so much from Michael. More than books will ever record. One thing I learned is how much precious time goes by in those first four years. Moms of babies and toddlers often have no idea how much their children are soaking in early truths about the love of God . . . even through a song! The sketch they later develop of both God and themselves can be dramatically colored by the crayons of influence they're given in those primary years. We wonder if we're wasting our breath on such young ears and don't see a correlation when our children develop an affection for God later. Our early encouragements are not guarantees, but when we lead them by the hand down the path, they'll know where to find Him long after they've let go of us. Mercifully, God makes Himself discoverable to those who search even if the jungle is deep and the path totally unfamiliar. He tenderly offers them His *own* hand. No, we didn't have our boy's plump little hand in ours for his first four years, but we held on as hard as we could for the next seven. Thank goodness, God holds on no matter what. Zephaniah 3:17 even says that He sings over us. Sing loud over my boy, Lord. Sing where he can hear you. We sang as long as we could. You sing now.

Our seven years with Michael brought many challenges, but we, too, had so many laughs and sang so many songs. Michael loved the "homemade" songs as well and also requested a few of them at school. His music teachers were no smarter than Amanda and Melissa's. The homespun songs were not his favorites, though. Neither were the "God-songs" as the children called them. The song he requested more than any other was a familiar lullaby: "Hush little baby, don't say a word. Momma's gonna buy you a mockingbird. If that mockingbird don't sing, Momma's gonna buy you . . ." We sang that song countless times. Even as a teenager no longer living in our home, he still asked me if I remembered it. I've sung it a time or two in the last several years . . . but not in the rocking chair. He's much too old for that now. He cherishes the memory and so do I. Long after he was gone, I mused what might make such a song a child's very favorite. Surely every child at one time or another yearns for his momma to give him something—*anything*—that will make everything better. Sometimes Momma isn't able.

Moms worry about the strangest things. As our children leave home, we're often inundated by "woulda, coulda, shoulda's." After our boy no longer lived within our four walls, I punished myself endlessly by thinking of every possible thing I might have done differently. The enemy is so mean, isn't he? He accuses us at our most vulnerable points where we are too emotionally involved to discern truth from lies. I regretted more than a few times that I had not insisted on our most repetitive song being something more meaningful. Something about the love of God, for crying out loud! He was the gift I most wanted to give my children. I was passionate about God being the most important, the most joyous, and, yes, the most *fun* part of our lives. Did I drop the ball at my third shot at parenting? Or the *hymnal?* Should I have done more, said more, even *sung* more?

As time goes on, I forgive myself a little more for not being a precious little boy's absolute salvation. That's God's job . . . but I sure wanted to help Him. From a personal standpoint, I am able to cling to one thing: I would have walked through fire if it would have helped. I know that. God knows that. I realized how deeply my heart was scarred when someone I love called my hand at remaining more distant from my friends' little boys than their girls. He was right. I was jealously guarding my heart so I would not betray my own boy of seven years or take such a risk again. I am not starting to forget, but I *am* starting to heal. Last year some of our best friends became grandparents. We all celebrated like crazy. We even talked to them in the delivery room by phone right after the baby was born. *It was a boy.*

I head to their house every time their grandbaby comes to town. They've even been kind enough to let me rock him back and forth in my arms a few miles. His mommy has done several of my video-based Bible studies in their home, so he seems perfectly familiar with my voice. He is a beautiful baby just like I know Michael was. As I held this little one, I couldn't help but think about my own little guy and the song he loved to hear as I rocked him. Before I knew it, I was singing it again. This time, however, I changed the words. *Just to be on the safe side.* No, I don't think one little song makes that much difference. But we don't get a thousand chances for a do-over. I took mine while I had it. That's my God for you. Ever willing to give the seeking a new lyric to an old song.

Hush little baby, Daddy's got a Word
No eye has seen, no ear has heard.
Dream sweet dreams but you can't dream this,
Plans your Weaver weaves for bliss.

Hush little baby, don't you cry.
Daddy fixes all things by and by.
Cease your striving, rest your eyes.
You're my joy and you're my prize.

Sleep little baby, I'll stay awake.
If skies should fall and mountains quake
You'll be safe in Daddy's arms,
Wrapped in blankets, robbed from harms.

Hush little baby, I will sing
While angels dance and 'round you ring.
If I should come before you wake
Your eyes will open to your Daddy's face.

So hush little baby, trust me now.
Thrones and powers to me bow.
I tell oceans what to do.
I think Daddy can take care of you.

He put a new song in my mouth.
a hymn of praise to our God.

PSALM 40:3

Me and my best friend.

CHAPTER 11

THE STRAY DOG

A house has an uncanny way of shrinking at exactly the same time the family within is growing. Keith and I had one child who was like one, one child who was like two, and another child who was like ten. Altogether that makes thirteen. Don't even try to reason with me on this one. There is no possible way we expended all that energy on only three children. I meet people who have raised and homeschooled five or six children and wonder what all the fuss is about over two or three. They are perfectly calm. They look like they've never missed a nap. Their children are well behaved, brilliant, and one another's best friends. I just want to slap them. But I'm too tired. My three wore me out.

I can remember days when every square inch of the house seemed to have a human appendage on it. Feet on the walls. Hands in the toilet. Heads in the refrigerator. Everywhere I looked was a person. Most of them called me "Mom." Nope. No way could there have been only three. Thirteen if there was one. I don't have an inkling how my mom managed five and kept a sound mind. Of course, no mom "keeps" a sound mind. The best we can do is realize early on that it's missing and find it pretty quickly. My mom lost hers often enough to leave her children a head full of quirky memories. After I had children of my own, I finally realized why my mom answered "Whatty" every time one of us called out, "Mom?" When we were little and incessantly chimed, "Mommy?," she developed the habit of responding in proper syncopation, "Whatty?" She kept it up until she died. She did the same thing in the grocery store even when it wasn't her own children yelling "Mom!" The memory of it still makes me laugh. I feel sure that when God called her name, she answered, "Whatty?" She always said she just had too many younguns for one mind to handle.

I've come to the conclusion that whatever number of children a mom has is a house full. Psalm 127:5 says of children, "Blessed is the man whose quiver is full of them." I don't doubt it, but *tired* is the woman. Her blessings come much later when her husband and children "rise up and call her blessed." She'll shed a tear or two then say, "And while you're up, would you get me a glass of water?" Or the salt shaker? Or some more cereal? Or the ketchup? Or any one of those jillion things they always asked us to get "while we were up." Somehow, I don't recall being anywhere but "up." I'm not complaining. The thought of a few innocent paybacks just makes me grin from time to time. I have made it clear to my household that if I'm ever infirmed and have to be transported in a wheelchair, I want a particular unnamed person I used to push in a stroller to have to take care of me. Then, when she has me at the mall and asks me nicely to cooperate with her about something, I'm going to throw myself out in the floor and have a screaming, kicking fit right there in front of everyone. Go ahead and admit it. Wouldn't that be a blast?

No doubt about it. Nothing is "fuller" than a house full of children. That's why the last thing a mother needs is another pet! Right about the time I was most besieged with parental challenges, a medium-size, nondescript black stray dog camped herself on my front porch. If she could have reached the doorbell, she would have rung it. As it was, she simply sat and waited. While the girls thought she was ugly, Michael, about six years old at the time, begged for her to stay. I was ordinarily fairly easy to talk into almost anything, but we already had a cat and a dog and far more than I could manage besides. I was adamant that the Moore house was not accepting another boarder with a mouth *or* fur.

If I was serious about not adding to our ranks, I should never have said, "If we don't feed her, she'll go away." Michael could turn an instruction inside out at mind-boggling velocity. He clearly reasoned, "If I *do* feed her, she will *stay*." I never once caught Michael in the act, but I assure you that stray dog was the most well-fed mouth at our address. Ignorant of my darling son's devices, I kept saying, "I just don't know why that dog won't go away." As if it happened yesterday, I can picture that innocent-looking face as he responded, "I don't know either. That silly dog is not very smart." Oh, but that boy was. No matter how many times I swept that dog from the front porch, she'd show up for an encore the very next day. One day when I was particularly put out (a term all mothers understand), Michael whacked me with the irrefutable: "Mommy, she's lonely. She doesn't

have a family. She wants someone to adopt her. Can *we?*"
What could I possibly have said . . . and still lived with
myself? It will not be a tremendous surprise to anyone who
knows me that I gave in. "OK, son, but I can't handle another
thing. You're going to have to take care of her, play with her,
and feed her." Suddenly, I was "the best mommy in the whole
wide world!" What we won't do to hear those words!

Michael named her "Sunny," and he quickly tagged her
as his best friend. From the start, nothing was ordinary about
Sunny. She obviously had roamed the streets most of her life.
She refused to stay in the house or the backyard. She could
practically dig through a brick wall. If it was all the same to
us, she preferred sitting right out front, and from there she
came and went as she pleased. Then one day she *went* and did
not *come.* Michael was devastated. I had to admit, I missed
her too. She was such company to him and just the mild-
mannered kind of pet he needed. We drove around the
neighborhood asking if anyone had seen a dog by that
description. I could hardly believe my ears when five or six
people said, "We have a dog that sounds just like that. She
comes and goes, but we love her, and the next time she shows
up, we're planning to keep her. She needs a home." It became
clear to me the smart little dickens didn't need a home, she
already had half a dozen. I suddenly felt like an idiot. I realized that the brilliant bag of fleas was holding tryouts. What
made me feel even more ridiculous is that I stiffened my back
and resolved to win. Michael and I walked to the next house
like Wyatt Earp and Doc Holiday on their way to the OK
Corral. We drew our fists and knocked on the door. The man
responded, "It sounds like you're describing our new dog. She

just came to live with us recently." About that time Sunny ran out of their front door and Doc Holiday fell in a heap right on top of her. Funny. Only a week or two earlier I was threatening anyone who fed her, and now I was making a fool of myself over her. Sunny had become the neighborhood pet, and everybody was claiming ownership. You know what they say about possession being nine-tenths of the law, however. By golly, we were taking her home or else. This showdown called for a secret weapon, and little Doc delivered it. He turned on the tears.

The man really hated to part with her, but Michael could wail the loudest of any child you have ever heard. So, off we went. Mother, son, and the smartest dog this side of the Mississippi. We had won the battle, but had we indeed won the tryouts? Clearly, convincing Sunny to move in permanently was going to take some effort. We put a plan into motion and aggressively commenced courting her favor. Sunny began to go almost everywhere with us. She and Michael were thick as thieves, but I was growing more attached by the day. It was interesting how much cuter she got once she was "ours" and we started falling in love with her. The same principle is why none of us parents know if our children are really cute or not. The way I see it, love is far more nearsighted than it is blind.

Then the day came that Michael no longer lived under our roof. His new home was very small, but it was full of puppies. Thank goodness he had "built-in" pets. The new litter made his transition easier, and I don't know what I would have done if he had asked to take Sunny. I might have held firm until he pulled out his secret weapon, in which case I probably would have given in. As it was, Sunny stayed. Maybe dogs have character enough to love the ones that need their attention the most. She didn't care how I looked, how I spoke, how I wrote, or how I produced. She was crazy about me. She was a wonderful caretaker, and I don't mind telling you that I needed care. Those were terribly difficult days, coinciding with the progression of my mother's illness, Amanda's impending high school graduation, some very painful personal crises, and the transfer of my best friend to another state. That silly stray dog and I became inseparable.

I don't want to brag, so I'll just try to stay with the facts. Sunny became the perfect dog—the best of everything you've ever seen on television. Even people who hate dogs love Sunny. She's never demanding. She's always attentive. She sits on my feet while I do the dishes. If I dig in the garden, she digs in the garden too. If we float down the river, she swims in front of me and pulls me on an inner tube. She prefers outside plumbing. She shakes hands. She loves nothing better than a road trip and sticks her face out the window, ears blowing in the breeze, making everyone smile who passes us by. When we use a certain tone of voice with her, she plops down on her belly and puts her paws over her eyes. She understands countless verbal commands. I'm telling you, this is Lassie dressed in black.

Years ago the boys down the street made fun of Michael because he was so proud of his new pet, a scraggly stray dog. I overheard them ask him, "What kind of dog is that stupid thing anyway?" He never hesitated. "A guard dog!" Indeed she was. *She still is.* For years, she sat right on the front porch until the last Moore was safely inside the house for the night.

When Amanda was in high school, she was often the last one in on a weekend night. Sunny would do a mental head count, come up with a sum of five Moores alive and accounted for, and follow her in. My heart nearly broke in two after Michael left. Night after night I went outside and said to her, "Sunny, come on in. Michael's not coming home for a long while." Before I knew it, I was out on the front porch again, this time saying, "Sunny, come on in. Amanda's not coming home for a long while." Then inconceivably, "Sunny, come on in. Melissa's not coming home for a long while."

Try explaining things to a dog that don't even make sense to a parent. These days Sunny is my best friend. When I'm out of town, she doesn't just sit on the porch and wait. She sits on the edge of the yard and stares at the end of the street, watching for my car to turn that corner. Keith tells me that if he wants her to come in while I'm gone, he practically has to carry her. The moment I drive up, she barks like crazy and darts like lightning across the yard, threatening anything that moves so I'll have safe passage. She has saved me from the birds at our bird feeder more times than I can count. You should see the feathers fly. No telling what those sparrows would do to me if Sunny took her eyes off of them. Peck me to oblivion, I suppose. I'll never know, though, because Sunny is ever there to deliver me from fowl play.

She's also right beside me to relate no matter what mood happens to have overtaken me. To have been created as technically unspiritual creatures, dogs have a lot less trouble applying Romans 12:15 than humans do. Dogs just don't have a problem weeping with those who weep and rejoicing with those who rejoice. If I'm sick, she lies on the end of the bed like she's nearly dead. If I'm sad, she sits beside me and sighs until I'm over it. If I keep crying, she finally turns to me abruptly and licks me right on the face. It gets a laugh out of me every time. If I'm mad, she barks like the dickens. If I'm anxious, she'll leave a path in the carpet from pacing back and forth. If I'm happy, she wags everything from her shoulders back.

Say what you want, but that kind of friend works for me every time. A cynic can make fun of me like the boys down the street made fun of Michael, but I'm going to tell you what I think. I think God planted that silly dog on our front porch eight or so years ago. Goodness knows, Michael helped God *keep* her there, but God got her there. Now, Sunny's not some kind of celestial being with invisible wings. She's just a dog. A mutt at that. But a mighty fine one. Like most of you, I have a complicated life. Lots of demands. Unimaginable stresses at times. People share things with me that could make a person unable to sleep at night. Life can take a lot out of a soul. Every once in a while God grants you something that just *gives*. That's my Sunny.

In Psalm 50:10–11 God Himself said:

> for every animal of the forest is mine,
>   and the cattle on a thousand hills.
> I know every bird in the mountains,
>   and the creatures of the field are mine.

If the cattle on a thousand hills belong to Him, so do the canines in a thousand yards. I'm so glad God chose to send one medium-size, furry black stray dog to our yard all those years ago. For the life of me, I don't know how we'd have gotten a cow in the car.

If you don't have any boys,
borrow some!

Christmas is best spent with
the best of friends.

CHAPTER 12

HE FRAGRANCE

"Can you believe how old I'm getting, Mo?"

"No, darlin'. I sure can't."

As I lived and breathed, that child's voice was changing. His fifteenth birthday just around the corner, he sounded like a young man on the other end of the telephone. Surely that couldn't be the pint-size four-year-old boy my husband "gave" me for Valentine's Day so many years ago. He had lived with us for seven years until his birth mother—a close relative—was ready to have her boy back. I could hardly believe a decade had passed since he first walked through our front door. I remember every detail of that night. He was the tiniest, most beautiful little boy I had ever seen. Plump face. Big round eyes the color of pecan pie and eyelashes that seemed to fan instead of blink. I could not believe he was "mine."

I so clearly recall warning Keith not to think of walking through the front door with that boy unless he was absolutely certain the child was ours to keep. "If I never have him, I won't know what I missed, but if he comes and I lose him, I'll be so heartbroken that I'll end up being sorry we ever did it. I won't be able to stand it." Oh, how silly we are at times. How little we know about what we can stand. How soon we forget that one of God's chief purposes for our continuance on this planet once we receive eternal life is to reveal His glory. More often than not, this noblest of goals is accomplished by showing that the "all-surpassing power" in our feeble jars of clay comes from Christ, not from us. Hard lessons to learn. I don't profess to know much *now,* but before Michael, I didn't have a clue.

I issued *both* Keith and God a list of requirements in order for me to agree to the impending arrangements. Let me rephrase that. I offered them a *deal.* Needless to say, the terms were all directly or indirectly established to protect *me.* I was neither aware of my self-centeredness at the time nor spiritually discerning enough to know anything was wrong with it. Don't you know God gets sick of our self-indulgent mortal tendency to interpret everything around us in terms that are "all about me"? Deliver us, Lord.

I don't mind telling you what God did to help "deliver" *me.* He did not fulfill a single requirement I gave Him. Never meant to. He intended to bring Michael to us for a season. We were oblivious. I had nothing but romance in my eyes. *Happily ever afters.* Utter certainty that *love will conquer all.* In retrospect, I think I had the audacity to think it was *my* love that could conquer. And God could help out when I needed Him. Trust me—I needed Him before I knew what hit me. That's one lesson I didn't take long to learn. In my prior—*albeit ignorant*—assessment, I really thought that if I was cut out for *anything,* it was loving children. All I needed was just the right conditions, and I made those very clear in advance. Like most things involving children, *none of those conditions were met.* In retrospect, God's unwillingness to meet the conditions was exactly His point where I was concerned. I had never in my life wholeheartedly practiced the essence of unconditional love. I would not have dared take such a risk. Keith would also have done whatever he could to protect me from such risk . . . *except* resist the urgent needs of a certain little boy in our extended family who "could really use a home." Keith's heartstrings struck such an irresistible chord that he had no recourse but to move to their impulse. Translation? Neither he nor God paid any attention to a thing I instructed them to do. I thought we had made a deal. Later I realized *we* hadn't made any such thing. The deal was mine. I did all the talking. And I shook on it. But I was shaking *air.* Somehow I had the weirdest feeling even way back then that no one was on the other side of that handshake.

From the very first stages of our "adoption" dialogue until now—a season spanning over a dozen years—I have encountered complexities of circumstance and emotions like nothing I've ever known. People who mean well ask questions about things they do not understand. I couldn't have understood it either unless I had experienced such complicated circumstances firsthand. I am fiercely and unapologetically private about it. I knew, however, when God placed the concept for this book upon my heart, that I could not possibly write about my children without writing about *all* of my children . . . even one who was only "mine" for a season. I find myself wanting to say to my reader, who has become like a friend through the years, "May I share this much without being expected to share much more?" Perhaps I am naïve, but I have to believe that she will draw from the well of compassion and her answer—*your* answer—will be *yes*. These are not easy things for me to share. Thank you for letting me impart them as I'm able.

I'm writing to say I am not sorry. Even after all the heart-wrenching pain, confusion, doubt, and disappointment—mostly in myself. Even after all the blood, sweat, tears, expended energy, defeated determination, utter exhaustion, and unanswered questions. And even after the most over-riding emotions of all, loving and losing, and the indescribably excruciating feeling of failure. It wouldn't do any good to try to reason a single one of these with me. They are for God and me to sift through piece by piece. What's most important for now is that what has been sifted from my home has not been sifted from my heart.

I am so glad the wind blew that little sparrow to my nest. And that, though the gusts were often hard and some-times blinding, they were not hard enough to sweep him out of our nest for seven years. *Seven years.* Somehow in that blessed number of completion, I've got to believe God required those years from all of us involved to complete a number of wonderful and eternally profitable works. Works that would otherwise have been unaccomplished. Hidden treasures that would otherwise have never been discovered. I'm still digging those diamonds one by one out of the rich soil of that valley. I pray that all the others involved have the same earth under their fingernails. My God is faithful. That

I know. And I will trust Him for what I *don't*. God never promised us *answers* in this lifetime, but He did indeed promise treasures to the seeker:

> "I will give you the treasures of darkness,
>   riches stored in secret places,
> so that you may know that I am the LORD,
>   the God of Israel, who summons you by name."
>
> (Isa. 45:3)

What I am about to write I have felt before, but I've not yet voiced it. It's been far too painful. It's a simple thing really . . . but the feeling is profound in my heart: I am so grateful for that little measure of time I got to experience being the mother of a son. Ah, yes. The mother of a man-child. Sometimes I wish God had purposed for all of us who have the desire to know the joys and distinct experiences of raising both a daughter and a son. I wouldn't have traded either for the other. If only for a short time, I got to experience both. And I loved it.

I grin as I recall some of the distinctions I never did take for granted. I *loved* folding little boy underwear. Oh, my. He will be mortified if he ever reads this! I loved seeing his cowboy boots sitting near his dad's. I loved blowing his hair dry and gelling it so it would stick straight up in the front like a crew cut. (I made sure he was the cutest thing ever to grace the doors of his school because he could be so challenging. I wanted them to think he was too darlin' to snatch bald headed.) I loved his size 6 camouflage coveralls matching his daddy's for surveying wildlife unaware. I loved how he preferred a hammer and nails to *painting* his nails, for crying out loud. I loved how he'd rather jump the curb with his bicycle than simply pedal it nondescriptly into the driveway. I loved how he'd say, "Oh, man! Look at that cool car! Step on the gas, Mom, and let's check it out!" And I would! I loved how he said to a little boy in our carpool, "You can come and live with *us*. They'll letcha." And most of all, I loved how he loved me. Oh, little boys do love their mamas. Even temporary subs. I loved how he would hug my neck so hard sometimes I thought I'd burst an artery. I loved how he'd look at me every once in a while with eyes sparkling like stars and say, "You sure look pretty, Mommy." And I'd *feel* pretty. In the midst of many hard times, we had some perfect moments. I have God's permission to keep those forever.

For anyone who hasn't had the distinct experience of parenting both a girl and a boy, don't despair. If you want, you can borrow one! I've done it for twenty-plus years. My best buddy and I met when our oldest children were nothing but babies. We taught Mother's Day Out together for several years and even planned to have our second children around the same time. Sure enough, they were born two months apart. Each the same sex as the older sibling . . . even after we had implicitly asked God for the other. So, what's a mother to do? Share! We each had those four younguns' at our houses more times than I could "shake a stick at," as my folks would say. Come to think of it, I believe I shook a stick at them almost every time they were together. Thankfully, I didn't have to use it. Our trade-off philosophy meant that my buddy has gotten to do all sorts of "girl things" with my daughters and I've gotten to do all sorts of "boy things" with her sons. God alone knows how many times I've been squirted by their water guns. Now that I think about all they put me through, I'm not sorry about the dog bite.

My friend's sons are second in my heart only to my children. I'm crazy about them. Their prospective wives will have to pass my tests as well as their mother's. Incidentally, the ministry has been such a shock to the boys. Years ago when my friend was director of women's ministry at a local church, I spoke at one of her conferences. Several days later the evaluations she had taken at the event were lying on her table. Her youngest son was in the fifth grade and he took it upon himself to read the evaluations. He demanded from his mother, "Are these things talking about *our* Beth?" When she answered affirmatively, he said, "I think she wrote all of these herself! Somebody's making all this stuff up!" We hooted and hollered!

He's lived long enough to change his tune, however. Just recently, he met some young women on his college campus who are doing one of the Bible studies. He told his mother that I was helping him "with chicks" and I didn't even know it. "Chick magnet," he called me. Have you ever? He's asked me a million times when I am going to mention his name in a book instead of just referring to the "fine sons of my best friend." OK. His name is Jordan. His older brother's name is Jeremy. They are handsome. They are hilarious. And they are half mine. *So there.* If you've never had sons or daughters, go borrow some! They're a lot less trouble! Johnnie's happy she doesn't have to buy for mine, and I'm happy I don't have to clean up after hers!

Practicing on my friend's boys helped me not be quite so shocked when I suddenly had one of my own. After two little girls, a boy can be quite . . . uh . . . *new!* I'll never forget taking Michael to the pediatrician some months after his arrival in order to have his ears checked. Before the exam, I pulled the doctor aside and confessed, "I'm afraid he has a hearing problem. I say things to him, but he doesn't seem to hear me." In retrospect, I think I recall a smirk on my pediatrician's face. Still, I was paying him the big bucks, so he performed a careful examination. Then he seemed almost proud to announce, "Mrs. Moore, nothing whatsoever is wrong with this boy's ears. He doesn't have a hearing problem. My unofficial diagnosis is that he may more likely have a *minding* problem. Welcome to the world of little boys." I was terribly insulted.

We had many difficult challenges but never as a result of the mere differences between girls and boys. I celebrated every single one of those diversities. To this day, few things ever happen in our family that I don't note how the girls respond and wonder how my boy would have responded. He weaves in and out of my thoughts continually. Even though there is much I don't understand, God has undoubtedly proved once again to be all wise. He used our little family to accomplish some important things in Michael's life and Michael to accomplish the incomprehensible in ours. But in His wisdom He knows that much of what He has yet to accomplish for all of us is through other means.

To some degree my friend's boys have helped ease the pain of no longer having a boy of my own. But as close as we are, they are their mother's sons. That's how it should be. One day I will have sons-in-law. How wonderful that will be! But no matter how many young men I have the privilege of loving, Michael's place in my heart is secure. And that's also how it should be. The wonder— from a personal standpoint with my personal history—is that *I don't mind.* I've come to understand that the spot in my heart that never loses its tenderness keeps me knowing it was real. That I really did take the risk. The ache is proof I let him in. Without a single one of my preliminary demands met. I loved him to pieces. Still do. And I am not sorry. These were huge tests for me.

I wasn't even sorry when the worst tidal wave of grief swept over me. Michael had been gone for about a year. I was sitting on the end of our bed, and I suppose I must have had that faraway stare in my expression that caused my husband to know the center of my thoughts. He sat down beside me, put his arm around me and said, "Honey, what is it?" Panic consumed me as I cried out, "I can no longer remember how he smells!" I don't know how to explain it. I will trust mothers, particularly those of sons, to understand. Little boys just smell differently from little girls. If I may smile through my tears, they smell sort of like a wet puppy. Sometimes I miss that most of all. Actually, that boys can have their own "out-doorsy" smell is perfectly biblical. I saw it not long ago in Scripture, and God and I had a sweet moment together. In Genesis 27:27, Isaac said, "Ah, the smell of my son is like the smell of a field that the LORD has blessed." I, for one, believe there were puppies in that field. *Wet ones.*

The fragrance of my boy remained for many months in my imagination as a feather in my nest. It no longer lingers. Still, every once in a great while, I will awaken from a dream and it is there.

Amanda and Melissa weren't the
only ones going in circles way back then.

CHAPTER 13

THE TREADMILL

Next time you see me, you may not recognize me. Just the other day I bought some wrinkle cream at Kroger that will start showing "visible signs of improvement in just fourteen days." I'm on day three. The product promises continued improvement, so by the time you and I happen to run into each other, I may look like I'm in my twenties. The label says a few drops will improve the appearance of my fine lines, but my problem is that I have a few lines that aren't so fine. In fact, a year or so ago, I looked in the mirror and I had on somebody else's neck. I don't know who she is, but I didn't ask for her neck. I want my old neck back. So I'm using more than the label says.

I'll tell you something else I need. *Knee cream.* No, not for the joints. I want wrinkle cream for knees because who-ever's neck I got also gave me her knees. And while we're at it, I stared at my hands the other day, and they're looking more and more like my mother's. I didn't stare for long. I was too scared that age spots would start breaking out before my very eyes. I'm sure that somewhere I read a book or article that gave me a thousand reasons why growing older is so much better. Right now I'm having a little trouble remembering about nine hundred and ninety-eight of them, but one thing I know for sure: looks was not on the list!

If I didn't already know, I'd demand that someone tell me who came up with all this aging stuff. What I *don't* know is what in the world God was thinking. If He's going to present me without spot or wrinkle, He better get this under control soon. Don't misunderstand me. I'm really not just skin-deep. I am thrilled that "inwardly we are being renewed day by day" (2 Cor. 4:16). It's the "outwardly we are wasting away" part that bothers me. With all my heart I want to be the Proverbs 31 woman, but for the life of me, I can't figure out why she's laughing "at the days to come." It's not *that* funny.

Maybe I know too much. The Proverbs 31 woman clearly did not have a bookstore nearby. After I turned forty, I announced to my best buddy that it was time she and I were more informed about our physiological future. After eating a high-fat, low-fiber lunch, we drove to the bookstore. We didn't consider walking. After all, the bookstore was four blocks from the restaurant. This time I didn't go to a Christian bookstore. I didn't want sweet people sugarcoating the facts for me. *"Just tell me like it is. I want the facts."* I sat in the floor of the "women's health issues" aisle and pulled out all the books on menopause. My plan was to choose the most informative one for purchase. My friend decided that if I wanted to learn the facts, I could do it alone. She hightailed her way to the Christian fiction section. "Fine," I said. "But you're not going to be prepared for the future."

Let me just go ahead and say, there is no way we're going to be prepared for *this* future. The news isn't good, girls. We stand to experience somewhere around thirty symptoms and side effects of this "very natural process," not one of which is vaguely tolerable. Or natural, for that matter! For crying out loud, what woman over forty wants to talk about what's natural anyway? And don't say a word to me about "mother nature," either. Nature is *not* a mother. That would necessitate her being a woman, and no woman would have come up with this. I'm about to work myself into a hot flash. All I've had so far is warm flashes, but my symptoms are coming so quickly, I have little doubt I will be fanning before I finish this chapter.

I wish I could say more on the topic. Goodness knows it would be cathartic for me. *But I'm not allowed to.* My oldest daughter happened to be in the audience of a group of women I addressed soon after my tragic ordeal at the bookstore. I was the slightest tad more graphic about what I had read. She was so mortified that I have been forbidden to go into any detail about it *ever again.* So, if you want to know, you'll have to do your own research. You'll never, ever force it out of my mouth. Just allow me to say that there are a lot of hair issues. I'm sorry. I didn't make the rules. But I am trying my hardest to find a way not to *keep* them.

I don't mean to be one-sided. I realize our male counterparts have aging challenges as well. It's just that I cannot remember for the life of me what any of them are. Now, let's see. Does ginseng help memory or is it estrogen? I don't remember that either. All I know is, my husband gets better looking by the day. He is so handsome with his *touches* of gray. I do not have touches of gray. I have been slapped silly by gray. That's the least of my worries, however. I pay big bucks for someone to deal with that particular hair issue. I'm not too proud to admit it. Poor, but not proud.

I'm here to tell you, we women live under a ton of pressure. And by some strange process indigenous to our gender, we translate every bit of our pressure into the most familiar five-letter word in feminine existence: G-U-I-L-T. Many of us (present company included) weren't under enough stress with our work *at home,* so we thought we'd add a little more with forty to fifty hours of work *at work.* But we really should be home more. *Guilt.* And we really need to do a better job at work. *Guilt.* We finally fit in a trip to the grocery store on a spare Saturday hour only to stand in a checkout line with a dozen magazines telling us how glamorous, fit, and professional we're supposed to be. There we stand in our sweats, no makeup, and our hair in a ponytail if we still have enough left. We've got enough groceries to give us a solid half hour of reading torture. We force ourselves to look at the other side counter. The one loaded down with treats. Do we grab a Snicker's bar or a magazine? *Guilt either way you go.* We'll just do our best to stare straight ahead. Then the checkout girl announces our total, and it's far more than we should've spent. We know we should coupon . . . but who has time? *More guilt.*

Goodness knows we try. That's what that treadmill is about. Now, don't you go playing dumb with me. You know the one. Sure, you may have already destroyed the evidence by putting it in a garage sale . . . but you haven't forgotten. It's the monument many of us keep in our houses as a reminder of all we're *not.* We didn't have room for it in the first place, but it's a necessity if we're going to "keep up." We'd put it in the TV room, but who could hear the television over all that racket? It looks a little odd in the corner of the dining room, but it's a good reminder at mealtime. Perhaps we should move it to the bedroom. That way, guilt could be our last thought at night before going to sleep.

Honestly, I really do like to take a walk several times a week if I can fit it in. It's just that I like to actually *go somewhere* when I walk. Something about working up a sweat going nowhere on a treadmill is too much of a picture of how we mortal creatures spend a significant portion of our lives. No thanks. Still, I hate to get rid of it. We may be in for a spell of bad weather that miraculously coincides with a sudden burst of energy. I may use it yet.

In the meantime, perhaps you and I could find some other household uses for it. After all, treadmills aren't cheap. They ought to be multipurpose. I've thought about putting it at the top of our stairs. The kids could pile their dirty clothes on it, and then when the load's nice and high, they could turn on the switch and shoot it downstairs to me. Our treadmill has a tilting action that makes this feature particularly feasible. The girls could even catapult one piece at a time while I stand at the bottom and catch. Any chore that enhances family unity is time well spent. My only holdup is that if my theory works as well with the dirty clothes as I picture it will, the kids might think to try the dirty dishes too.

I have a feeling God wishes a few thoughts would occur to us. One of the childhood images that has stuck with me all these years is the Jetson cartoon clip where George is stuck on the treadmill, long skinny legs flying, and he's yelling, "Jane, get me off this crazy thing!" All these decades later, I feel sure

Jane couldn't help him because her legs were flying out of control on her own. Don't you know God looks at us running ourselves into a frenzy and says, "You're sure not doing all that for *me*. I didn't get you into this mess." In a couple of different places in the Book of Isaiah, God looked upon them in their captivity and basically said, "I'm not the one wearying you, but you're about to weary Me" (Isa. 1:14, 43:24, my paraphrase). Can't you imagine God sees our misery with our worldly identity and wishes we would take Him at His Word?

You see, while I was gathering feathers from my nest, I found a few of my own. Tail feathers, that is. From the years I'd run my tail feathers off trying to measure up. I am a long way from having all these worldly stresses and strains licked, but I'm also a long way from the place I used to be. No, I'm not crazy about the physical effects of aging . . . but I am happier and more comfortable in my own (looser) skin than I've ever been. Not only that, like many of you, I live under unbelievable pressure, but actually, I am calmer and more peaceful than I've ever been.

The time release on my ginseng must have just kicked in because now I suddenly remember one of those nine hundred and ninety-eight reasons why growing old is better. Sometimes we've allowed God to use the time to teach us a little more sense . . . regarding what's most important in life, for starters. I can't give you a single encouragement on this aging stuff, but I have learned volumes about finding a schedule you can live with. Boy, have God and I spent some study halls covering this one. I was no different than a lot of Christian women. I knew enough to put a priority on God's approval, but what would be the harm in having everybody else's too? After all, "everybody else" tended to be a lot less understanding than God. I cannot tell you how much I wanted to be all things to all people. In fact, the pure attempt nearly killed me. The more I studied God's Word, the more I realized how much I'd unintentionally bought into the world's myths. I'd like to suggest two myths that keep us trapped on a treadmill going nowhere:

Myth #1: We can do everything well. No, we can't. Not only that, God never told us to do *everything* well. He said that whatever we do, do it all for the glory of God (1 Cor. 10:31). The more God has a say in our "whatever," the more we'll be able to do our "all" to the glory of God. The treadmill setting goes from "aerobic" to "maniacal" when we are bound and determined to do a thousand things. Not only is it impossible to do a thousand things well; we certainly can't do a thousand things to the glory of God. But we *can* . . .

- seek Him each season of our lives,
- discern His present priorities for us,
- pour our priority energies into those things, and thereby,
- do them to the glory of God.

No mortal filled by the Spirit of God ever wanted other believers to fulfill their callings more than the apostle Paul. I love his Holy Spirit–inspired words in Philippians 1:9–11: "And this is my prayer: that your love may abound more and more in knowledge and depth of insight, so that you may be able to discern what is best and may be pure and blameless until the day of Christ, filled with the fruit of righteousness that comes through Jesus Christ—to the glory and praise of God."

Paul *knew* what God prioritized for him. He didn't try to do Peter's job, or Barnabas's job. He did not go everywhere he received an invitation. When the Spirit compelled him to go, he did not remain with a group of people no matter how much he loved them or how they begged him not to leave. No telling how he disappointed his parents and failed to meet the expectations of friends and associates, yet when his life was nearing its end, he was able to say, "I have fought the good fight, I have finished the race, I have kept the faith" (2 Tim. 4:7). Plenty of people had not yet heard the Word, but Paul understood that the whole world was not *his* responsibility. It was *God's.* No matter what was left undone or how others rated his success, Paul knew he had finished his race to the satisfaction of the One who summoned him to the track. He had one primary goal: "If only I may finish the race and complete the task the Lord Jesus has given me" (Acts 20:24). His take on life in every season was "forgetting what is behind and straining toward what is ahead, I press on toward the goal to win the prize for which God has called me heavenward in Christ Jesus" (Phil. 3:13–14).

Paul's prayer for us in Philippians 1:9–11 suggests that it is just as possible for us to discover and fulfill our own individual callings as it was for him. God's favor is upon all those who seek Him, not just a chosen few. We won't ever take the challenge out of life, but great relief and satisfaction can come from seeking God's priorities for us in each season, discerning what is "best" in the midst of many noble opportunities, and pouring our most excellent energies into those things. Which reminds me of the futility of the second myth.

Myth #2: We can make everyone like us and approve of us. A great and profound word comes to my mind on this one: *Baloney.* We will never, no matter how we try, become all things to all people in our lives. To try eventually makes both them and us miserable. Moses' father-in-law phrased it beautifully when he saw his son-in-law's vain attempt. The King James Version of it makes me grin: "The thing that thou doest is not good. Thou wilt surely wear away, both thou, and this people that is with thee" (Exod. 18:17–18). In other words, our overactivity and overresponsibility not only hurts *us;* sooner or later it will hurt others too. Jethro advised Moses to fulfill *his* primary God-given purposes and to allow others to fulfill those remaining.

Just as God had primary responsibilities for both Paul and Moses, He has them for you and me. We will *surely wear away* both us and the people that are with us, as Jethro said, if we become a slave to the needs and desires of others. I'll warn you in advance. You will get untold flak for prioritizing God's revealed and present will for your life over man's but, boy, is it worth it! Galatians 1:10 asks a critical question: "Am I now trying to win the approval of men, or of God? Or am I trying to please men?" Paul then spoke of the total futility of attempting to please both: "If I were still trying to please men, I would not be a servant of Christ." Simply said, we become a bond slave to whomever we try to please. I'll stick with Christ. In comparison to the unbearable load others will gladly place on us, His yoke is indeed easy and His burden light. I have discovered that when I please Christ, I end up inadvertently serving others far more effectively. When I seek to please others, I forfeit the pleasure of Christ and can't get others to "stay" pleased anyway.

Not too many years ago, I was almost ready to collapse both physically and emotionally under the weight of pressure I felt. I could see myself becoming more and more imprisoned by the religious world's demands. You see, the approval of the outside world isn't my present temptation. The approval of the "inside" religious world is! The expectation level honestly became cruel and unusual punishment. I'll never forget coming to the realization that a frightening portion of the religious world would not mind demanding more and more from me and many others in ministry, drawing us further and further from our spouses and children; *but* they'd also be the first to judge when our marriages fell apart and our children rebelled with resentment, wondering how a person in ministry could have let such a thing happen. It just doesn't pay to strive for the world's approval, whatever our "worlds" of temptation may be.

Would you like to know what helped me break free? I finally became so exhausted and frustrated that I told God if He'd give me a prescription for deliverance, I'd take it! His prescription? "Do what *I* tell you to do. Nothing more and nothing less. No matter who disapproves. Obey me and I will unload your burden." I desperately sought discernment to recognize the rule of thumb God had for me at that season and He graciously gave it. I heard Him very clearly speak these chief purposes into my heart: "I want you to pour your priority energies into your immediate family and to the ministry I've given you." And I surrendered. Before you get any lofty ideas about how it all turned out, a whole lot of things have been left undone. I stay behind on my correspondence. I disappoint somebody virtually every week. More often than I wish, it may even be a cherished extended family member.

I don't keep up nearly as well with my outside relationships as I wish. I rarely talk on the phone. I say no far more often than I say yes, sometimes to things I'd really love to do. To my benefit and theirs, I spend an average of four nights a week with no one but my family members. If anything's left after my priority energies have been poured into my family and the ministry, I do something extracurricular. Otherwise, I have very little social life. Now, don't go thinking this is God's expectation for you too. He is a very wise, very personal God. He will tell you what He wants from you just as He told me. Ask Him for discernment to recognize His best for you and the courage to obey at the risk of others' disapproval.

God spoke an adamant word to me based on 2 Timothy 2:4: "You will be much less frustrated when you accept the fact that you are not a civilian." I have accepted that. So, am I miserable and bored, all work and no play? Hardly. Thank goodness my family and my ministry staff are great fun! I take considerable criticism at times and it still hurts . . . but would you like to know something? I'm content and at peace. Keith has had a wife. The kids have had a mom. Exhaustion and stress come and go, but they do not rule my life. For now, I have made it my goal to please Christ. I certainly have not arrived, but His joy is my pursuit and I have discovered that when I am obedient, He shares His joy with me, just as He promised in John 15:11. I'm not saying everything else is unimportant. I'm just saying that I've learned to see everything else as optional.

God has the sovereign right to adjust the rule of thumb for my life with every season. For instance, just because I don't get to do much mentoring one-on-one during this season doesn't mean I won't next season. That's entirely up to Him. Until then, no matter how much pressure I get to please people or how often I may feel the sting of criticism, God reminds me of a powerful portion of Romans 14:4: "To his own master" a servant "stands or falls." Christ alone is our judge . . . and He loves us more than He loved His own life. You don't have to worry about "measuring up" to Him. Your worth was measured on the cross. Our identity is in Him alone, and anything this world has to say about us contrary to His Word is a lie. Recently I heard a fine young preacher named John Durham say, "God's Word is not only an *autobiography of Him*. It's a *biography of you!*" How true! And how awesome! While you're finding out what's true of Him through His Word, find out what's true of you too! Your *real* identity is going to blow your mind. No matter what anyone else thinks of you, dear one, God thinks so much of you. Find out how much.

These truths mean *everything* to me. How I pray you will be encouraged too. God has a present will for your life. It is neither chaotic nor utterly exhausting. In the midst of many good choices vying for your time, He will give you the discernment to recognize what is *best*. Ask God what few things He desires you to do wholeheartedly to His glory, then do them, and don't let others add to them! It's time to get off that treadmill, sweating and striving and getting nowhere. No wonder we feel old! Let's figure out the goal then press on toward it!

One of these days we're going to finish our race. Until then let's throw aside a few encumbrances and let God free us up to feel the joy of a little cool wind in our faces as we run (Heb. 12:1). Yep, my race has gotten a little easier since I cast aside some of the weights others handed me. But I'm still a long way from making it onto the cover of God's version of *Modern Maturity*. Why? Because while I'm running the race, I still wish my knees looked better. And I'd just as soon my neck wouldn't flap when I run.

Incidentally, my children tease me pretty unmercifully at times about that old treadmill that still gathers dust in the guest room. I just smile and bear it because I know something they don't: that silly monument to all I didn't become and couldn't pull together was a monumental choice made in their favor. And, anyway, they're almost grown now. I may be just about ready to rev the thing up.

Writing this reflection has really been good for me, but I'm still going to keep using my wrinkle cream. For heaven's sake, I can't stop now! I'm just eleven days from a visible difference! What if it doesn't work? Whatever do you mean? It's got a money-back guarantee! Of course, I realize they're banking on the fact that we won't march up to the counter, demand to see the on-duty manager at Kroger, hit him with our purse, and say, "It's been fifteen days. Now, take a good look at these wrinkles. Do they look any better to you, mister?"

Anyway, we've got heaven. Sooner or later, we'll be looking good. You can act like that doesn't matter to you if you want. If it's all the same to you, my new life verse in the midst of menopausal madness may become Philippians 3:20: "But our citizenship is in heaven. And we eagerly await a Savior from there, the Lord Jesus Christ, who, by the power that enables him to bring everything under his control, will transform our lowly bodies so that they will be like His glorious body." New necks. New knees. No spot or wrinkle. That and Jesus too? Blessings all mine with ten thousand beside!

At peace after a furious storm.

CHAPTER 14

THE MAGAZINES

If we adults think the pressures of the world are almost unbearable, we don't have a clue. Most of us have enough years on us to recognize that we're spinning out of control, to locate the negative power source, and to pull the plug on the treadmill if we're serious enough about changing. I am completely convinced, however, that Satan has launched a full-scale attack on our young people that is so shrewd, powerful, and encompassing they don't even know what has hit them.

I was painfully reminded of one dimension of it recently when I came across a stack of old fashion magazines. Not all feathers left in our nests provoke happy memories. One of the things I like best about God, however, is that He can redeem absolutely *anything*. The family memory I want to share with you in this reflection is not a pleasant one. I choose to share it because it's an *important* one. While I can't say that I'm necessarily glad to have had this feather in my nest, I wouldn't trade the precious little sparrow that left it there for anything in the world. Furthermore, I wouldn't trade what God redeemed out of this one "feather" for a whole handful of happier ones.

I am alarmed about our young people. I wish I could tell you that my alarm has come strictly from what I've seen and heard through my travels, but that's not true. While what I've seen "out there" among our youth would be enough to scare a soul half to death, I know more than I ever wanted to know *firsthand*. Satan came calling for my own children. He not only wanted to disable any potential they had to make his life miserable, he also wanted to get to their parents. Satan knows that one of the most effective ways to get to any of us in ministry is to get to our children. He got my attention all right. Then *God* got my attention. The devil didn't get the full victory he wanted in those battles, but neither the girls nor I would mind telling you he left them pretty bloody.

Satan tailors his schemes to fit his subject; therefore, my girls' battles took on different forms. Amanda discovered the vivid reality of Jesus Christ through her own personal difficulties. Thankfully, Satan never got far enough with her to threaten her life. I want to share a little bit about Melissa's battle with you because hers had the potential to be deadly. Yes, I mean that it literally could have killed her. She is just one of untold thousands of otherwise sound-thinking, successful Christian young women who have fallen into this life-threatening brand of Satanic snare. Melissa is very vocal about her experience and passionately desires that Satan be exposed. I not only have her permission to share this, I have her encouragement.

I'm going to allow Melissa to share her own story with you through an excerpt from a paper she wrote for one of her college classes. She is one of the gutsiest young women I've ever met, willing to let herself look weak so that God's strength can be revealed and the devil can be defeated.

It was homecoming, the biggest event of the year for a high-school girl. I was getting ready for the football game. This particular year I was up for homecoming queen, and my dad was there to escort me down the football field. The four other girls and I were anxiously waiting for the life-or-death call.

I had on a Georgiou suit for the occasion and a very expensive formal for the dance. I had an appointment with a makeup artist and manicurist before the dance. I had spent tons of money at a tanning salon hoping that the tanning beds could make me look better. I was the size that I wanted to be due to the fact that I had not eaten in months. I was everything that Hollywood was telling me that I had to be. I was deathly skinny, popular, and completely miserable.

The morning after the event was over, I woke up to the smell of warm blueberry muffins. I walked downstairs only to see the norm. My mom was sitting in the dining room doing her "quiet time." Her "quiet time" was the time she spent alone with God each day. Without catching her attention, I watched her. She was in her old, faded pink robe. Her hair was a mess, and she did not have on a hint of makeup, but she looked so beautiful.

I had watched her do her "quiet time" for seventeen years, but it had never caught my attention like this. There was something about that day that was absolutely brilliant. Her face was radiant. I saw her sitting there in her chair and knew that she was truly satisfied. I wanted what she had. She was confident about who she was, even without makeup on. I envied her. I wanted to have whatever it was that fulfilled her.

I tiptoed up the stairs and dug around in my drawers. Finally, I found my own dusty Bible I had shoved in the drawer every Sunday after church. As I cracked open the Bible, I felt immediate renewal. I felt that I had some kind of energy somewhere deep inside my soul. I flipped through the pages and read words that I did not understand. But I knew that they meant something powerful. I could feel the power. I remember staring at a verse that told me who I was in Christ. It said that my body was not my own and that my body was the temple of the Holy Spirit. I found that my identity was in Christ, Himself. That was refreshing to me, because I hated myself.

I looked up from the pages of the Bible to the walls that surrounded me. I felt instant oppression. The walls were covered with magazine cutouts of Elizabeth Hurley and Kate Moss. The walls were overlapped with pictures of women that resembled skeletons. I tacked these on my walls to remind myself that I was forbidden to eat and that I was fat. I would not pass the pictures without a deep feeling of worthlessness and shame.

A few minutes later I heard my mom walking up the stairs. She said, "Melissa where are you? What are you doing?" The tears streamed down my face. She wrapped me up in her arms and read me the words of

King David in Psalms. The words gently soothed my
ears and my heart. One by one, my mom and I ripped
off the magazine pictures. I bitterly threw the pictures in
the trash and walked away in agony. I spent the rest of
the day trying to differentiate between who the world
wanted me to be and who God wanted me to be. I sat
at the computer and typed out Scripture and printed it
out. I replaced the bare walls with God's Word . . .

It was a parent's worst nightmare, and it barreled out of
control so fast, our heads were left spinning. Melissa was *not*
a troubled child. She was a deeply loved, very well-adjusted
child who had received countless accolades for her successes
in all sorts of areas. She was a darling size 6 who couldn't have
cared less how many French fries she ate. Then suddenly,
through a toxic cocktail of just the right conditions, her little
world started quaking. The first I realized the pressure girls
her age were under was a year or so earlier when I took both
her and her sister to a nice mall in Houston to try on prom
dresses. I took two completely happy, well-adjusted size 6
daughters into the mall, and two hours later left with two terribly depressed teenagers who were convinced they were fat
and ugly. I was so mortified over the mannequins in the windows that I finally checked the dress size on one of them. It
was a 2. The girls seemed to forget the trauma over the next
few days, but I never could get the experience out of my
head. A red flag started waving, but I also knew I had to be
careful not to overreact or try to overly control them.

Time passed without any real signs of oncoming trouble.
Melissa had quite an eye for putting clothes together and had

decided she wanted to be a fashion design major when she entered college. She began looking through more and more fashion magazines. I grew concerned and started dialoguing with her about them immediately. I always had to be careful about how I dealt with Melissa. She was one of those kinds of children who could have knee-jerked with total rebellion if we forbade her every single potential hazard. Her weight and her attitude remained steady and visibly unaffected, so I just continued to watch and pray. Then something unforeseeable happened.

About two months before the events she described in her paper, someone very dear to Melissa moved literally to the other side of the world. She was absolutely heartbroken. Melissa is much like her mother in that she doesn't just love with her heart. She seems to love with her whole being . . . so when she gets hurt, she hurts all over—*heart, soul, mind, and body.* With indescribable alarm, Keith and I began to watch our gregarious child sink under a cloak of despair. The lower her spirits sank, the less appetite she had. Soon everything made her sick to her stomach. Weight began rolling off of her like snow melting under a sudden summer sun. We immediately took her to doctor after doctor. We never could get a physician to diagnose her with what we suspected. Each one independently diagnosed that she was depressed over the difficult losses she had suffered over the recent years. Her brother had returned to his birth mother, her cherished grandmother had died, and her big sister had gone to college. They each felt that her friend's departure had triggered a full-scale physical, emotional, and mental response to the cumulative losses. Keith and I concurred with their diagnosis, but we also felt that it was leading to an eating disorder with a potential much deadlier than depression.

Here is the mind-blowing part of this scenario. While we were trying to tell Melissa how sick her precious little body was and how it was starving for food, her peers were telling her how fabulous she looked. I cannot estimate the amount of praise she received for being physically ill. Our precious young people have been totally brainwashed by the media. Pictures on magazine covers that have been doctored and airbrushed to look utterly perfect have become their ideal. How in heaven's name have we been talked into buying "perfectionism" from such a grossly imperfect world? In one form or another, it's happened to all of us. The difference is, our children are too young to fight it off for themselves. They need our help. And not just their parents. They need the help of the educated, joyful, trustworthy, and Christ-confident adult believers who will expose the lies and tell them truth. Still, many may choose not to listen, but God will hold us responsible, as the adults of this generation, to tell!

I urge you not to think for a single moment that I have become an expert on dealing with teenage depression or eating disorders. *I have not.* I would advise anyone in the same frightening situation to do the same thing we did: mobilize and seek sound, godly counsel and proper medical attention. I am far from an expert on eating disorders, but I have learned a few things about warfare in my time. Keith and I chose good doctors and counselors and let them do their job. *Then we did our job.* We fought our heads off in prayer and drew our swords like crazy, battling the enemy with the Word of God. In the power of Jesus' name, we absolutely refused

Satan any right to destroy our daughter's life. Thank goodness, we had Melissa's cooperation! She wanted to get better.
She did not want to be captive to a stronghold and, to the
glory of God, the child did practically everything we asked
her. You see, no matter how Keith and I loved her and fought
for her, a measure of the battle was hers alone to fight. We
could teach her how and support her in prayer, but we
couldn't "make her" do what the furious battle demanded.

Many of the Scriptures in the chapter of *Praying God's
Word* called "Overcoming Food-Related Strongholds" were
those we prayed over her and she prayed over herself. She
used them so much I had to laminate them. I believe that a
key to the victory God soon had in her came from her willingness to forsake her pride. I gave her a list of Scriptures that
I had personalized by inserting her name in them and
instructed her to pray them every day. I never in a million
years expected the child to take them to high school with her!
I would have thought she would have been too afraid someone would discover them. Not only was she unafraid of being
"discovered," she came home to me one day and said, "Mom,
I'm going to need a new set of Scriptures. I shared mine with
a friend at school who needs them so badly."

When Melissa pulled down the pictures of the bone-thin
models and replaced them with Scripture, she was unknow-
ingly performing a vivid demonstration of 2 Corinthians
10:5: "We demolish arguments and every pretension that sets
itself up against the knowledge of God, and we take captive
every thought to make it obedient to Christ." She tore down
their pretension of perfection and the arguments they raised
against the truth of God's Word.

Those magazine pictures said something to Melissa contrary to what God says about her. When she tore them down and replaced them with the knowledge of God, she demonstrated in physical terms what we're to do in spiritual terms: take our thoughts captive and make them obedient to Christ. If she had stopped with the physical demonstration, little would have changed. Instead, she began to practice spiritually what she had done physically. She started allowing God's Word to expose the lies she had believed, and she began writing down and believing what He said about her instead. The change didn't come overnight. Change in habitual thinking rarely does. But God used the process of time to do far more than an instant healing would have accomplished. She learned to trust Him, love Him, and depend on Him.

That's when the most amazing thing of all happened. The little that Melissa knew about God and His Word started whetting an appetite in her that she couldn't quench. She pleaded with me to tell her how I came to love Him. She asked me questions about His Word constantly. She studied portions of Scripture then asked me to listen to her thoughts on it to see if she was interpreting it correctly. She got into in-depth Bible study and went through *Breaking Free* with a group of college girls. Her thirst for God began with desperation but developed into delight. Just like her mother's did. And just as it did for ten thousands of others who have been captured by the healing heart of God.

David was one of those. Psalm 18 is a testimony of his love for God. It is the only psalm David began with the words, "I love you, O LORD, my strength," as if bursting at the seams to testify. To me, his approach seems to suggest he couldn't wait to work up to a crescendo. The psalm literally began with his compulsory confession of intimate affection. Because of my own experience, I have no trouble imagining why David loved God so. The words immediately following his outburst of love say volumes: "The LORD is my rock, my fortress and my deliverer; / My God is my rock, in whom I take refuge. / He is my shield and the horn of my salvation, my stronghold." Somewhere along the way, the God of the universe—his father's God, and his grandfather's God—had truly become *his*. Their relationship became deeply intimate in a spiritual sense, somewhat like the two described in the Song of Songs: "I am my beloved's and he is mine."

I watched the same thing happen to Melissa. God was no longer just her mother's intimate partner. He became *hers*. How? Perhaps David said it well for both of them in the very same psalm: "He reached down from on high and took hold of me; / he drew me out of deep waters. / He rescued me from my powerful enemy, / from my foes, who were too strong for me. / They confronted me in the day of my disaster [in other words, they took advantage of David's weakened state, just as the enemy took advantage of Melissa's after her loss], / but the LORD was my support. / He brought me out into a spacious place; / he rescued me because he delighted in me" (Ps. 18:16–18). I have watched God perform a staggering miracle. Before my very eyes, over the course of a year, He took her disaster and used it to teach her delight.

Her lessons in passion still continue today. No, I don't know about tomorrow, but I have to believe that what she learned in her "yesterdays" will help draw her home in her "tomorrows." Melissa is a very young woman and has plenty of battles in front of her, but she has a victory behind her that sent Satan into a tailspin. For now, the child is head over heels in love with Jesus. Her Bible looks like it's been through the dishwasher. Melissa knows where she's "been had" and has to live on her guard constantly. She may be vulnerable to the same attack for many years, but at her young age she has encountered a God more alive, active, and powerful than she ever imagined.

The girls were very young when the Holy Spirit struck the match of passion in my heart for God through His Word. I began praying constantly that God would do the same for my children. More than I prayed for their well-being or blessing, I prayed for them to love Christ and His Word with all their hearts. Like their mother, they have a long way to go and lots of growing to do, but God has begun to answer my prayers. And I'm here to tell you, watching Him do it has been excruciating at times. More than worth it, but excruciating. I came upon a verse the other day that beautifully expresses what a parent goes through during a process like the one I've described. Galatians 4:19 says, "My dear children, for whom I am again in the pains of childbirth until Christ is formed in you, . . ." Parenting is *painful.* Like stages of labor, at times the pain is more intense than others, while in between there are intervals of peace. *I want Christ formed in my children.* Like the Galatians to whom Paul was writing, my children are already Christians. Paul didn't mean he wanted the Galatians to be saved. He wanted Christ's personality, character, and activity to literally be formed in them. That's what I want too. If you're a parent or a grandparent, that's what you probably want too. What you and I have to realize is that the process at times will be like going through the pains of childbirth all over again! But the character of Christ developed in them will be worth it! We have to be willing to labor in prayer and battle enemy forces with God's Word as He allows affliction, temptation, or tribulation to prompt a growth spurt. And all the while, we've got to be careful we're not getting in His way! We can't do it for them, but we can pray that they won't be able to resist Him.

Our young people are under severe spiritual attack. They are living with a totally different dimension of warfare from their predecessors. The Word explicitly teaches that Satan's fury will be increasingly unleashed until he meets his final destiny. Revelation 12:12 helps explain the alarming rise in destruction and wickedness: "He is filled with fury, / Because he knows that his time is short." He specifically targets young people for a host of reasons, not the least of which is because they "have their whole lives in front of them." They are also tremendously vulnerable.

Satan is attacking them with every conceivable device to demean and disable them. They are dealing with addictions and compulsions of all kinds. They have easy access to unimaginable pornography. Incomprehensible lyrics pound their way into their brains. Stunning numbers of *Christian* teens are saying the same words Melissa testified to in her paper: "I hate myself." Oh, how that breaks my heart! Many are dearly loved children who have been affirmed all of their lives. That's how powerful this present darkness is! The scream of the world is deafening and blinding them. It is time we start speaking louder than the world. Not just with our words but with our lives . . . and on our knees.

Satan has no right whatsoever to captivate our Christian young people. He's getting away with it because the home and the church are letting him. He *wants* us to buy in to all this talk about the "lost generation." He knows the exact opposite is on the horizon. What I believe he fears is the fulfillment of Acts 2, that this same generation of young people has a potential to rise up with an affection and an anointing that may be beyond anything we older folks have ever witnessed. He's scared to death of what would happen if they broke free from their bondage to the world. He's doing everything he can to offset the powerful anointing he knows eventually will fall by disabling potential threats while they're young.

The church, by and large, is failing to address Satan's assault on our children. The oversight isn't intentional. We just haven't yet awakened to the magnitude of the problems assaulting our kids. To complicate matters, masses of Christian parents leave most of their children's spiritual education to the church. Many have good moral homes based on Christian principles, but based on what I'm seeing, "good" by itself is not going to cut it anymore. Our teenagers are desperate for parents with tenacious spiritual savvy who are willing to war for them and teach *them* how to war. If we don't know how to war, God is so willing to teach us. That's what He did with Keith and me, and continues to do as we meet new challenges. Satan would love for us to lose heart over how little we know and how ill equipped we feel. Christ simply wants us to come to Him and learn! "Take my yoke upon you and learn from me" (Matt. 11:29). Keep in mind that spiritual tenacity is developed. As Psalm 18:34 says, "He trains my hands for battle."

The urgency of the situation necessitates that we move from *reactive* to *proactive*. As it is, most Christian homes are relatively spiritually passive, counting on the church to give their kids the tools they need. Even if the church is stepping up to the plate and doing its job where young people are concerned, a Christian teenager may spend 5 or so hours out of a 168-hour week under its influence. Presuming a typical adolescent may eke out an average of about 7 hours of sleep a night, that leaves 114 hours at the mercy of the world's propaganda through peers, various kinds of education, and every kind of media known to modern man. No, I'm not suggesting we try to snatch our young people entirely out of the world. Christ coined it perfectly in John 17:15 in His intercession on our behalf to His Father: "My prayer is not that you take them out of the world but that you protect them from the evil one."

Bingo. We've got to teach them how to take God up on the divine protection His Word and His ways extend to them. They need our help. And I'm not sure they know enough to ask for it. What they won't take willingly, they can't stop prayerfully! We must *say on* and *pray on!* Becoming proactive rather than reactive takes tremendous courage and holy sweat, but look what we stand to gain: children who are overcoming the schemes of the evil one and developing the pure character of Christ. Which of our children has not been worth the labor demanded to birth them? How much more so will the pain of childbirth be worth it, until Christ be formed in them?

O, God, train our hands for war and teach us how to train our children. They have wandered onto the most violent battlefield in human history, but most don't know it. Few of those who are aware know how to use their weapons. Lord, open our eyes to the urgency at hand. These are precious lives with inconceivable godly potential. Please arouse a righteous ire in us. Summon us to their sides and enable us to assist them in their fight against this powerful foe. Greater are You, Lord, who are in us than he who is in the world! You have equipped us with divine weapons for the demolishing of strongholds. Satan cannot wage a battle against believers that we cannot win. It is time, O Lord, it is time. Break the bonds on the wrists of our children then turn their faces upward, that when Your mighty anointing falls forth from heaven, they will be baptized by power and consumed by holy fire. Do not ease Your hand until You have made each one a threat to Satan's purpose. Heap upon Satan's own head a double portion of what he tried to heap on theirs. Raise up an army, O God. In the mighty name of Jesus, Amen.

Look up, children, for your redemption draweth nigh.

A wide open mouth
from the start . . .

I spent much of our lives
trying to cover it.

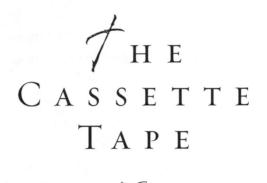THE CASSETTE TAPE

When our children were little, Keith and I were sure we had them pegged. Like lots of parents, we stereotyped them from the start. "Amanda is a carbon copy of her mother, and Melissa is a carbon copy of her father," we used to say. Translation: Amanda was (1) afraid of her shadow and (2) very diplomatic in her relationships. Melissa was (1) frightfully deficient of healthy fear and (2) never had a thought she didn't vocalize. Yep. One was her mother. The other was her father. We knew what to expect. Case closed. Then they had the nerve to squirm right out of that "case" and start breaking the genetic rules. While still maintaining much of her mom's take on life, Amanda began developing far more of her daddy's reserve and his preference for smaller, more intimate groups of people. The waters of her soul run deep, and she's a wonderful listener whose favorite ministry style so far is one-on-one, much like her father. Melissa, a delightful

Daddy's girl, staggered her father's imagination when she developed a love for scads of people and could make a new best friend in five seconds flat. She is willing to share whatever she's learned (and a few things she hasn't) with whomever will listen, much like her mama. But you'd better be ready to hear what she really thinks because, like her daddy, she still has a rare thought she doesn't lend considerable volume.

Both our girls have turned out to be interesting concoctions of the two most diverse people the Lord Jesus may ever have pronounced man and wife. If either girl finds herself on a psychiatrist's couch one of these days complaining of an unexplainable sense of inner conflict, I can explain it: The parts of Keith and me inside of them are having a fight. And I'm sorry. I'm sure he is, too, but he'll save his admissions for a smaller, more intimate group of people. I'll just go ahead and tell everyone who will listen. All I know to tell my daughters is that their father and I not only learned to get along; we eventually became one another's biggest fans. "Just wait ten or fifteen years, girls, and everyone inside of you will start liking each other much better. You'll see. Until then, there's gonna be a war in there."

As free as Melissa has been with her art of expression, when she was about ten years old, I happened on proof that she really *did* have the ability to hold her tongue if absolutely necessary. Like, for instance, in matters of life and death. In the old days, I used to record cassette tapes of various high-energy Christian contemporary songs I owned so that I could listen to them for motivation while I exercised. The kids loved the tapes, too, and I often had to fish them out of their rooms. One day while I was putting clean clothes away, I found an old favorite tape stuck way back in one of Melissa's drawers. I couldn't wait to pull on my sweats, grab my hand weights, throw that tape in my player, and head out the door for a vigorous walk. I pitched the clean clothes and took to the street.

It was a blast. The weather was crisp and beautiful and the music was sublime. I turned the volume up as loud as I could stand. The words to the songs filled my soul, and I sang right with them at the top of my lungs. Too bad my neighbors couldn't hear the accompaniment. I've been known to put both my weights in one hand so that I can lift up the other in praise while I'm on my walks. Sometimes the neighbors make their children come inside until Mrs. Moore passes by. The day I found the old tape was one of those days when they would have shut the miniblinds.

I was caught up in praise and worship, pumping six pounds of iron to beat the band, and making a joyful noise when all at once the music on my homemade tape was interrupted by a terrible racket. The noise had the familiar ring of a novice trying to make a recording. I listened carefully as it became clearer and clearer that someone had recorded over my tape right in the middle of one of the best songs. The tape picked up sounds made by someone fiddling with the buttons on the recorder, then sighs of exasperation, and finally a little voice that said, "There. Now I can get started." I immediately recognized the voice of my youngest daughter. As many things as I had heard her say, nothing could have prepared me for what came next. She commenced to speak her mind on some matters she'd wisely chosen not to pursue with me. My eyes grew as wide as saucers and I stopped dead in my tracks, listening to my ten-year-old give her mother the "once over." She drew a breath and then she gave me the twice over. She had it out with me right there on tape. I can no longer remember what decision I had made with which she begged to differ, but I assure you, she did not mince words. My chin hit the ground as I heard a mouthful of things most kids threaten to say to their parents but prudently resist. I could just see that child standing in the middle of her bed, hands on her hips, "sportin' a proper tude" with that head tilting side to side, taking a breath only long enough to say, "And another thing. . . !" Only my Melissa would have recorded her thoughts for future listening pleasure.

Before you think I was terribly appalled, keep in mind this was my second child. Not my first. The truth is, I doubled over and laughed so hard that I had to roll in the grass in one of my neighbor's front yards. She even called her dog in the house. For all I know, she may have wanted to call the police. I would love to have explained my behavior to her, but I had a sneaking suspicion she wouldn't have "gotten" it. From all appearances she hadn't had a good laugh since 1972 and didn't look to be in the mood for a fresh encounter. Picture me saying, "You don't understand! This is my daughter telling me off! It's just hilarious!" Picturing the expression on Melissa's face and what her body language must have been like as she told me off made me laugh so hard I cried. What I would have given to be a bug on that wall when she was making her debut recording! As soon as I could pull myself together, I made a beeline right back to my house with the grass still clinging to my sweats. I called my mom and shared every word of it with her. She laughed her dentures off. I didn't say a word to Melissa about finding the tape for years. I don't doubt, however, that when she got off the school bus that day, I had a very suspicious smirk on my face.

The tape certainly wasn't a punishable offense. She hadn't liked my decision that day she made the recording, but she had obeyed me. I didn't ordinarily demand that my children act ecstatic about decisions they didn't like or understand. I preferred they be respectful, and I certainly expected their obedience, but Keith and I let them voice a measure of their displeasure if we could see they needed to be heard. I feel like God's that way with us at times. I don't always like His decisions, but when I choose to obey Him, the act of obedience still "counts" with Him even if I'm not thrilled about it. On occasion I feel like God has said to me, "Kick and scream all you want. Go right ahead and have a fit. Then when you're finished, do what I've asked you to do." Sometimes I said the same thing to my children.

Melissa talked big, but she almost always ended up doing what I asked. I remember a few times when I had to respond with a no to something she desperately wanted to do and she threatened, "What if I do it anyway?" I am so grateful that she was the kind of child I could answer like this: "Baby, you won't. Because even though you're mad at me and you don't like my decision, you are a child who obeys her parents, and I have confidence that you will do what we've asked." Sometimes I'd hold my breath and pray my head off, but she rarely let me down. She'd kick and scream and have a fit, but in the end she almost always did the right thing.

I happen to think God's not terribly offended when we do something similar. The *last* thing I'm recommending is telling God off, but I don't think an occasional fit under dreadfully strenuous circumstances is terminal. I'm not talking about a tantrum lifestyle. We'd be little more than childish *brats.* I'm talking about those times when we want God to move in a certain way or grant us something so badly we can hardly bear it, and He simply and emphatically says no. Something *important* to us. Maybe even a matter of life and death concerning someone we love. Or maybe what we want is something He granted to "so and so" but has withheld from us. Sound familiar? That can be as frustrating to us as it is to our children when their friends get things they don't. We can be so devastated over a divine ruling that we want to throw a fit. At the risk of sounding like a heretic, I'd like ever so gently to suggest that we might consider having one. It sure beats shutting down spiritually or turning our backs on the things of the faith. Since there's no way to have a fit behind God's back, I believe He'd just as soon we throw it right there in front of Him, dumping our frustrations and disappointments right into His lap.

Life isn't life without some divine decisions that our mortal minds simply cannot comprehend. At times, we cannot imagine why God couldn't have just given us what we asked. Sometimes our frustration lies in the fact that we know He *could have,* that He certainly had the power, but in His divine wisdom, He chose not to. Please hear this with your heart:

God knows we can't think like Him. His ways and His thoughts simply are not ours (Isa. 55:8–9). Sometimes the very essence of faith is trusting God in the midst of things He knows good and well we cannot comprehend. Not that we *won't,* but at times we literally *cannot.*

Having children of my own has given me far more insight into God's decision-making position. Some of the most difficult moments of parenting are those times when we must make a decision regarding our child that he or she *cannot* understand.

When I was fifteen years old, my family moved from a small town in Arkansas many miles away to the biggest city in the South. Our last afternoon in town, my best friend and several of our other buddies were supposed to take me out for a farewell lunch. We were loading the moving van when they pulled in the driveway. I ran to tell my parents that I was leaving for a little while, and they uncharacteristically refused to let me go. They tried to explain to me that the van was almost loaded and we were very close to our departure time. They didn't want to have to wait on me once everything was ready. "But we planned this! What difference does an extra hour make?" I begged but they wouldn't budge. I cried and cried . . . then I was so angry, I hardly said a word all the way to Texas.

My parents did not ground me or chastise me. There really was no need. I was not disrespectful. I was *angry* . . . and although I was trying hard not to voice it disrespectfully, I still *felt* it. Scripture implies that disrespect is always sin but feeling angry isn't. It's what we do with our anger that determines its transgression. My parents knew that I legitimately could not understand their decision. I simply lacked the maturity.

Inconceivably, far more was involved in their unwillingness to yield to my pleas than even they could have known. Unbeknownst to us until the next day, my precious friends suffered a head-on collision just minutes after they pulled away from my house on their way to the restaurant. One was injured terribly and two were killed. One of them was my best friend in the whole wide world. The one with whom I had shared a locker, tons of clothes, and countless "spendovers." I *still* miss her, and I have yet to fully understand the divine implications of what happened that strange day. I have, however, matured enough to trust that while God is always God, He's also always good. One day we formerly finitely minded earthlings will see Him face-to-face and know as we've been known. Until then, He does not mercilessly punish us because we *don't* know what we *can't*.

If my parents knew the difference between a punishable offense of disrespect and a legitimate lack of understanding accompanied by anger, how much more does our Father in heaven? If we're about to burst with feelings of disappointment and anger, they need to find a safe release. Otherwise, the lid on the pressure cooker is going to hit the ceiling. If we do nothing but internalize them, keeping the lid on tight, the water in the pressure cooker will eventually evaporate, leaving the pan hollow and empty. Emotions we have not poured out in the safe hands of God can turn into feelings of hopelessness and depression. *God is safe.* Psalm 62:8

says, "Trust in him at all times, O people; / pour out your hearts to him, / for God is our refuge." *At all times.* Not just when we feel nice and have lofty things to say. To me, the psalmist's inspired words give us permission to pour out *whatever* is in our hearts. If we're full of anger and disappointment and do not find a healthy way to pour them out, how in the world will renewed feelings of joy and peace find room? If we neither give our overwhelming emotions to God nor internalize them, our only other option is to spew them on others who are ill equipped to handle them.

In Psalm 64:1, David, the man after God's own heart, said, "Hear me, O God, as I voice my complaint." In Psalm 142:2, he said:

> I pour out my complaint before him;
> before him I tell my trouble.

Job, a man God held in high esteem, said:

> If I say, "I will forget my complaint,
> I will change my expression, and smile,"
> I still dread all my sufferings. (9:27–28a)

God can take our complaints. Even if they sometimes target a decision He, himself, has made in our behalf. Yes, God is the almighty Creator of heaven and earth and the righteous judge of the living and the dead . . . but He is also our Father. Our Abba. I love the words of David in Psalm 103:13–14:

As a father has compassion on his children,
    so the LORD has compassion on those who fear him;
for he knows how we are formed,
    he remembers that we are dust.

God undoubtedly commands respect, but I believe with all my heart that we can wrestle with Him over a decision He has made, voice disappointment, and maybe even blow a little steam without descending into outright disrespect. He knows we are dust. And, frankly, sometimes dust *blows*. I am utterly convinced that one of the keys in times of conflict with God over the humanly incomprehensible is learning to wrestle *with* Him rather than *against* Him. If we'll keep wrestling the matter through and continue to dialogue, even when our mouths are filled with endless "whys," we'll be like Jacob who wrestled with the angel in Genesis 32. The darkness *will* finally end, the sun will rise, and the blessing will most assuredly come. Weeping may endure for a night but joy comes in the morning (Ps. 30:5).

God knows in advance that some of His decisions are not going to be popular with His children. Still He insists on His way because He knows beyond a doubt what is best. Ephesians 5:1 says, "Be imitators of God." We are so wise to seek and follow His example in parenting, as difficult as the challenge may be at times. Let's admit it. The pressure to please our children can be overwhelming. Trust me on this one: I've given in a few times when I shouldn't have, but those times I allowed God to help me stand my ground were to my children's benefit *and* their eventual acceptance.

Sometimes the worst thing we can do is "give in" to the endless pleas that are intended to wear us down. Adolescents can be like termites that eventually eat up an entire house one bite at a time. Parenting takes pest control. That's all there is to it. Those to whom popularity is extremely important might want to avoid parenting. I have done very few things in life that have ever demanded the pure, long-term tenacity and courage of being a mom. It takes more guts than riding the Sky Screamer at Six Flags over Texas. And just about the time you shake off the last ride and get your wits back, you have to buckle yourself back in and ride again. Dear frustrated parent, when there is no other good news in sight, allow me to give you at least one piece: they *will* grow up. Until then, maybe this might help:

I learned something about biblical love almost ten years ago that helped me tremendously with my parenting. The Greek New Testament uses forms of the words *agape* and *phileo* to label kinds of love. Both are wonderful, biblical expressions of the heart, but when a distinction is drawn between the two, the difference can steer us significantly in relationships. When the scriptural context shows a distinction, *phileo* can often be understood as a love based on *common interests.* It is the love between friends or those who share a common bond like brothers and sisters in the faith. On the other hand, *agape* is a love primarily based on *best interest.* When Scripture speaks of God's love for His children, it almost always refers to *agape* love. God's love for us undoubtedly prioritizes what is in our best interest. While I desperately want God to be my friend and think of me as His, what

I need more than anything is a courageous heavenly Father who will look after my best interests even when I'm too near-sighted to recognize them. That's what our children need from us too. They need courageous parents who are willing to insist on their best interest even when they don't understand. Even when our decisions won't make us popular. What our culture refers to as "tough love" falls under the category of *agape*. Sometimes tough love is in the best interest of a terribly and repeatedly rebellious child. Our children don't need a buddy. They need a parent. Sometimes we have to be willing to *love* our children more than we're desperate for them to *like* us.

Yep. Parenting has taught me aplenty. And I don't doubt it will continue to. I pray that some of those lessons keep coming through unexpected amusements like the cassette tape Melissa recorded. Keeping a sense of humor is critical. If you've lost yours, then ask God for another one. I don't think He's running low. In fact, He and I shared a grand guffaw just the other day. A sister in the faith whom I've never met decided recently neither to entrust her angry feelings to God nor to keep them internalized. She opted instead to spew them onto a multipage letter and send them to me. I suppose it was appropriate since I was the source of her displeasure. Suffice it to say, she didn't like one of my ten-week Bible studies. And she had only finished *Week One*. I've considered changing addresses before she finishes *Week Two*. Even after her insistent coaxing, I couldn't concur with her on most of the letter, but she and I came to absolute unity on her prolific summation of my writings. She simply said, *"So many words, so little said."* It's not that I'm immune by any means. Harsh criticism really *can* hurt me. But I so wholeheartedly agreed with this one, I had to take another roll in the neighbor's grass.

No, I didn't write her back. But perhaps I could record a teensy little tape.

Amanda (far right)
and the best of Brownie friends.

How could this have
happened so quickly?

CHAPTER 16

THE GREEN CAP AND GOWN

"Mom, do I look OK?"

I was frantically getting ready for one of the most important days in our lives. I was torn between a thousand thoughts and a thousand tasks . . . putting dirty dishes in the sink and thinking how unfitting the menial seemed on such a profound day. I turned around to see what Amanda was talking about and there she stood. *In her cap and gown.*

Gulp.

Flashback. Over twelve years earlier, she stood in exactly the same place in the kitchen. My hands were in the same sink, elbow deep in Ivory Liquid. A higher, more childlike voice asked, "How do I look, Mommy?" I turned around and there she stood. *In her Brownie Scout uniform.* I fought as hard as I could not to burst into tears *or* burst into laughter. For the life of me, I couldn't decide which I needed to do most. She was the cutest thing I thought I had ever seen.

Grinning ear to ear with a mouthful of missing teeth. The little brown beanie sat slightly off center on hair still gold from the bleach of a hot Houston summer at the neighborhood pool. Her brown dress was identical to the one I had worn as a first-grader not so many years earlier it seemed. My relatives constantly spoke of how much Amanda looked like me as a child. Right at that moment, I could see it myself. I was six again and looking straight into the mirror on the inside of my parents' closet. And as my grandmother would have said, I was "lookin' right good." So was she.

"Let Mommy grab a couple of bobby pins, and I'll help you keep your beanie on while you do lots of playing today."

She stood up nice and straight while I pinned it on each side. I may as well have been pinning on a crown with the regal look of respect she had on her face. Respect for all the beanie stood for, no less. She wore her sash proudly draped over the proper shoulder. She still wore it proudly when her patches were put on with a glue gun rather than sewn on like the rest of her troop. I was never much for sewing, but I was Hoss Cartwright with a glue gun. I shot anything that wasn't standing still. To this day, all the figurines in my small Lladro collection have a telltale ring of clear glue around their necks. Keith, Melissa, and Michael were hard on the figurines. Thank goodness for my area of expertise. If only the Brownie Scout patches had glued on as well as the figurine heads. Instead, on a humid day they curled up like potato chips. And Houston is big on humid. By the time she earned all her patches, she looked like she was wearing a bag of Fritos. Now look what you've made me do. I feel guilty about it all over again. It hurts me to talk about it. I just hope Amanda's not scarred over it. Come to think of it, her mother is. You ought to see the scar I have on my knee from getting burned by that wicked thing. I was willing to make the sacrifice, and I'm not sure anyone even appreciated it. That's motherhood for you.

Amanda's grandfather made up for any shame cast upon her Brownie experience by her mother's ineptitude with a needle and a thread. She never failed to be the clear winner in cookie sales. And what could have been more important? My father-in-law ran a rather large business, and he took her cookie order sheet to work, implying to all his employees that he was signing paychecks on the back of it. I've never seen a group of grown men so fond of cookies.

Flash forward twelve years. "Oh, darlin'. You look absolutely wonderful."

"But am I wearing this silly cap right?"

"You sure are. It just feels awkward, doesn't it? Believe it or not, I remember. Let me grab a few bobby pins, and I'll show you how to pin it down." I hurried to the bathroom and dug a couple of pins out of the drawer. I glanced in the mirror and thought, *Hang on, old girl. You can do this.*

"Hold still, baby." I pinned the cap on each side. "You know, your cap and gown are exactly the color of your eyes. I'm so glad you went to this high school. What a shame to have had to wear some other school color that wasn't nearly so *you*."

She grinned. Because the statement was so *me*.

"I love you, Mommy."

"Oh, baby. I love you too." My heart just bled.

She hurried out the door to ride ahead with her friends. Many of them had been in Brownies together. Time may have flown by, but it had left its mark. They surely didn't look like Brownies *that* day. They were stunning. Still laughing and squealing, but this time they had all their teeth.

Keith and I arrived insanely early to the auditorium to make sure we had a bird's-eye view of the stage. I did OK until someone talked to me. But people just kept talking to me. Actually, I exercised no small amount of restraint. I acted far from what I *felt*. I *felt* like throwing myself in the aisle and rolling myself to death down the stairs. We got there so early, however, we were only five steps from the ground floor. No telling how many times I would have had to start all over on the fifth step and roll down until I finally succumbed. Amanda attended one of the biggest high schools in Texas, so goodness knows the graduation ceremony would have provided ample time and arguably even a little motivation for slow suicide.

As it was, I behaved myself and Keith patted me reassuringly. Melissa, who was seated with us, provided brief respite from the emotional wringer, as I intermittently had to whack at her for yelling and waving at her friends across the auditorium during the ceremony. Melissa is many things, but she is perhaps above all a distraction . . . no matter what the environment or who she happens to be distracting. That day, and countless others, I was just as glad.

As I stared at that vast sea of green caps and gowns, I kept thinking, *Wait one minute! How did we go from a Brownie Scout uniform straight to this?* The truth was, many a uniform had come in between. Amanda had played all sorts of sports, and I thought she was wonderful. She rarely pleased herself, however, and after a game often said, "I played terrible. And, Mom, please don't tell me that I looked precious in my uniform either."

"OK," I'd say, "But that's what I'm thinking." I drove my children crazy.

They survived. Well enough, in fact, it seemed one day they were Brownie Scouts and the next day they were graduates. The years in between seemed to pass in the blink of an eye. Still, as I looked at my firstborn from a distance in that auditorium, I knew she had learned so much amid those two twirls around my kitchen. Time comes and goes but, thankfully, never so fast that it doesn't do its job . . . if we let it. What a good job it had done through the hands of Him who holds the times. She had learned that the world was big and it could be awful. But not so big that one committed soul couldn't make it a little better. She certainly had made *mine* better.

In her mother's biased opinion, she could do almost anything well, but even her worst critic couldn't have denied the child could put pen to paper. I kept almost every paper she wrote between Brownies and graduation. No matter how old she got, however, she could hardly improve on the essence of life she captured in a paper she wrote in early grade school.

Her class was learning how to use adjectives. The teacher's instruction was to write a paragraph using as many descriptive adjectives as possible and expressing a scene so vividly that the reader could visualize it. Allow me to share Amanda's. She wrote it about one of her favorite places in the world: Waller, Texas, of all interesting venues. A one-light town where her great-grandparents had a small farm. The people were wonderful, but the exquisite beauty of the place was indeed in the eye of the beholder. Remember! Don't just read. *Visualize.*

My Trip to the Country
by Amanda Moore

My trip to the country was very refreshing. After the first thirty minutes we were really into the limits of the noiseless, colorful county of Waller. After the drive through the lovely county limits we came into the crop-filled country. Immediately we drove by a deep green grove. It looked like I was in Ireland. [Trust me. Ireland, it's not.] *Just minutes later the gorgeous pecan trees were on the right side of the crossroad. Overhead were swarms of vultures, for a dead armadillo was laying on the side of the road. On the way back home we saw vast herds of horses and cattle. Our trip was very refreshing!*

If that isn't life, I wouldn't know it if it hit me. Right there in your journey down the road of life's most picturesque seasons—just when it all looks as if you're on the bonny green hills of Ireland—leave it to life to throw a dead armadillo into the scene. Just as sure as we get life like we want it—the country *crop-filled,* the grove *green,* and the pecan trees *gorgeous*—we no more than glance up and the vultures are circling. And why? Another armadillo is dead on the side of the road. Only a youngun' raised in Texas could have captured the essence of life's unpleasant interruptions with a dead armadillo. Around these parts, no sooner has one been scraped off the road than another waddles ignorantly to the same unfortunate demise.

The way I see it, Amanda's fine grasp of reality suggested that life is what we make of our dead armadillos. The interruptions to our picturesque scenes. Those aggravating times when we had life just like we wanted it and something had the guts to mess it up. Just keep in mind that we're doing OK as long as the only roadkill is the armadillo. Pardon the expression, but the point is that no matter how difficult a stretch of the road gets, we can't get down and "waller" in it. We've got to keep moving. Otherwise the vultures are going to circle overhead for more than the armadillo. If we're willing, God will produce a crop on that next stretch of road unlike anything we've ever seen in our deep green grove.

Amanda simply said *in her words* in grade school what the sons of Korah said *in God's words* in Psalm 84:

> Blessed are those whose strength is in you,
>   who have set their hearts on pilgrimage.
> As they pass through the Valley of Baca
>   they make it a place of springs;
>   the autumn rains also cover it with pools.
> They go from strength to strength,
>   till each appears before God in Zion . . .
> O LORD Almighty,
>   blessed is the man who trusts in you. (vv. 5–7, 12)

The word *baca* means tears or weeping. Though the Valley of Baca was an actual location in Palestine, the imagery the psalmist used in this sojourner's song is unmistakable. When life gets hard or we simply feel "worn to a frazzle," as my grandmother would say, it's time to take a deep breath and remind ourselves this place is not our home. We're just passing through on our way to a heavenly Kingdom. We are pilgrims here. The supply of "strength to strength" implies the demand. In other words, as long as we're here, we're going to need it. And as long as we need it, God's going to supply it.

When God first called me to speak and teach, I was a very young woman with almost no biblical knowledge and little experience. I am not a youngster anymore. I have lived plenty of seasons by anyone's standard, but I have yet to live a single one that was completely unchallenging. Even my seasons of refreshment and comparative ease still present daily pressures and stresses. I kept thinking a time would come when I'd get the knots of my past untangled and I'd breeze my way through the rest of life promising never to get myself in trouble again. I was wrong. I learned what you've probably learned. About the time we get the knots of our past untangled, the dangling strings of our ever-stressful "present" start tangling into knots of their own. I used to think that only people who had made lots of mistakes like me had really challenging lives and that all our troubles were simply consequences of sin. Wrong on that one too. Life is simply hard. That's all there is to it. Thank goodness, the intensity of difficulty rises and falls. Some seasons are far more bearable than others but none is without challenge. That's what the psalmist was talking about.

For every challenge, there is strength and if we're willing to receive it, something amazing can happen. Our Valley of Baca can become "a place of springs." My translation? Our seasons of tears can become the source of our deepest well-springs of personal revival. In fact, I'm hard pressed to remember many times my personal seasons of renewal did not spring from a valley of tears. I am so grateful to love and serve a God who offers favor to every pilgrim passing through Baca. I'm reminded of the line out of the timeless hymn, "Great Is Thy Faithfulness." Because God is faithful, He ever extends to us "strength for today and bright hope for tomorrow."

Of course, Amanda already knew all this. She just used a little different imagery. After all, life had pitched her straight from the bliss of Brownie Scouts into the bitterness of third grade. She'd see many an armadillo before trading in her uniform for that green cap and gown. Life won't let us stay in Brownie Scouts either. As much as I hate to be the one to say it, life just ain't all about cookies. If we live long enough, we grow up whether we want to or not. The good news is, we really *will* graduate. For those of us who trust in the *Lord Almighty*, this road we're on ends in an unimaginably spectacular place where armadillos never die and vultures never circle. From the tip of Mount Zion, we'll finally have the vantage point of seeing all the twists and turns of our journey as one ingeniously mapped means to a magnificent end. At that glorious moment, we're going to grasp why our roads took the turns they did and why some of our ideal moments were invariably interrupted by harsh realities.

Looking back on it, it won't seem nearly so bad. In fact in Romans 8:18, the apostle Paul says that we won't even be able to compare our sufferings to the glory God will reveal in us. That was his way of saying that the "end" won't simply be worth the "means." It will be inconceivably incomparable. Our synopsis of the trip will be sun-washed gold by the light of eternal glory, and somehow we'll look back on the whole thing, nod with new perspective, and say, "Our trip was very refreshing!"

Amanda got her diploma that day. In fact, she walked across that stage without my throwing myself down the stairs a single time. The vultures were circling all right. But to their dismay, we all survived. For our hearts are set on pilgrimage.

The five of us: Keith, Beth,
Amanda, Melissa, and
Beth's hair on Easter Sunday, 1987.

CHAPTER 17

BIBLES, BAPTISM CERTIFICATES, AND OTHER SIGNS OF CHURCH LIFE

Having unoccupied rooms for the first time in my life suddenly lent the invitation to get rid of a few mountains of accumulated junk in closets and drawers. I don't know how I possibly could have unloaded a mound of junk the size of Mount Rainier and still have the Rockies safe and secure at our address . . . but I did. My dilemma was that I happened on so much I couldn't throw away. One thing is for sure: I couldn't possibly let go of all the Bibles. It's too bad I feel that way since we've got enough to open our own bookstore. Every conceivable assortment. We have the *Precious Moments Bible,* at least a half dozen of *The Children's Bible;* we have the first Bible our church presents to children when they enter grade school. We have *The Family Bible, The Teen Bible,* and *The Student Bible.* You name it, we probably have it.

From the time our children were preschoolers, we taught them to carry their very own Bibles to Sunday school and church. In our own way we were trying to help them develop an understanding that God's Word is for *them* and that the older they got, the more they would understand how to hear from Him. Now don't you go thinking we were smarter than we were. Anything we did right was, as my grandmother would say, the "pure-dee mercy of God." Since carrying a Bible to church was nonnegotiable, the children approached us with their proposals for the *kinds* of Bible they would take. Hence, the collection. That was fine with us. We are so blessed to live in an era when Bibles are published with study notes for virtually any season of life. We just want them to love the Word and sense God personalizing it to them in countless ways.

As I stared at the mountain of Bibles, I thought of all the things it represented to me. God has used His Word so powerfully in this former captive's life that I cannot begin to recount its manifold influence. The stack of Bibles and the mental images of them clutched in my children's small hands reminded me of *church.* A place of familiarity to my children—and many others—second only to their home.

I love church. Not just my church. I love all sorts of churches. Red or yellow, black or white, and especially those rare and wonderful cornucopias of them all. Congregations of the lovers of God who have received salvation through Christ whether the sign on their door reads Presbyterian,

Assembly of God, Methodist, Baptist, Lutheran, Catholic, or anything else. I am a sister to all who receive the grace of Christ through faith. I have no idea how I could possibly have received such a mercy gift of privilege to worship with all sorts of colors and denominations, but I am the richer for it. In my experience and to my great delight, our sad stereotypes have far more often than not been proved wrong. Sure, we have different practices, but when we are willing to approach one another's observances with purified, open hearts, we will so often find God. Sometimes in the least expected places.

At the risk of disturbing someone who, incidentally, may *need* disturbing, I have knelt with Lutherans, said "Our Father" with Catholics, danced among the children in their circles of praise with the charismatics, and experienced the powerful worship of a quieter awe with Presbyterians. And that's just for starters. I have stood to my feet and waved my handkerchief in affirmation to fine preaching with my African-American brothers and sisters in Christ. I have gently bowed in respect to Chinese brothers and sisters on their native soil in Southeast Asia. I have yet to find a perfect church or improve upon its imperfections in the least by entering the midst. But I have yet to meet a grace-saved people that I could not appreciate in one way or another. I pray I'm far from finished.

I attend, love, and serve the home church of God's choice for me, but I am blessed immeasurably by *all* those who have bid me welcome, whether spoken or unspoken. *I love church.* That's all there is to it. I love what it stands for. I love its refuge for the needy. I love its shelter in the storm. I love its shade for the children. My heart is overwhelmed by passion as I make this plea: Oh, that our children would be offered the gift of Jesus first and foremost, but that they would also experience the intended gift of His church. His bride. The one for whom He died. How deeply God wants us to understand that when we receive Jesus, we are also offered the bonus of so much more! Romans 8:32 says, "He who did not spare his own Son, but gave him up for us all—how will he not also, along with him, graciously give us all things?" Among the first things meant to come "along with Christ" was surely His bride. That blessed entity that we automatically become a part of by *name* when we receive Christ but that which He desires we also become a part of by *practice.* By association. *By community.* Upon our salvation we are automatically granted the gift of belonging. The bride or body of Christ is the worldwide family of God, associated by salvation through Jesus Christ. But you and I were meant to discover the *firsthand effects* of her community through a warm and inviting local church.

This reflection is a brief but unapologetic apologetic for raising kids to be involved in church. I'm not talking about a certain denomination. I'm talking about any vibrant, Christ-centered, Bible-believing local church where "family" comes to mean far more than an isolated few who share the same mailbox. How grateful I am that many who never cast a single shadow over a church threshold in youth later receive Christ and become mighty men and women of God! Can we ever thank God enough for so mercifully pursuing us even when we knew very little about pursuing Him? But to be raised in church! What a gift!

Let me share just a few reasons—beyond the more obvious—why being raised in church can be such a gift: the connection to wonderful people of all ages—from the nursery to the elderly—they would never have otherwise known. Relationships with people who know them all their young lives. The same people who write recommendations for colleges and places of employment. The influence of strong and godly men and women. The priceless influence of peers making good choices in a hard world. And who can estimate the aid a community of believers can be to a single parent? Oh, I believe in church! The real kind. Not just the kind that gathers on Sundays. The gathering of fellow believers as you celebrate the marriage of your children. The gathering of believers in the waiting room as you sit through the excruciating hours of a loved one's surgery. The gathering of believers as you bury your dead. I believe in meals brought to the bereaved. In collections taken for the poor. In ministries to the shut-ins. In monies given to missions.

I believe in children's choir. In darling white robes and bright red bows. In risers full of children opening their mouths to sing of their Creator. Indeed, "from the lips of children and infants / you have ordained praise," O God (Ps. 8:2). My heart is moved with parents who cry as they watch carefully and listen for their child's own voice . . . for nothing is more precious than hearing the name of God's beloved Child fall from the lips of your own. And I believe in men and women who give countless time and excellence of effort to teach the young how to praise.

Several years before she saw the Lord, my mother told me something I hope I'll always remember. She arrived at her church earlier than usual for a discipleship class she was taking. She entered the church through the children's wing that would be bulging with children participating in children's choir in a little less than an hour. The hall was dark and all the rooms unlit except for one. As she walked past the one lit room, she saw a woman kneeling in the center of the room, surrounded by a semicircle of ten pint-sized empty chairs. My mother's voiced cracked with emotion as she described the fervent prayer this precious woman was voicing on behalf of a handful of children so young many would not even consider the job significant. Can you imagine how blessed those young children were to have been taught to sing praises by someone who brought forth her gift as if she were offering it to the King Himself? Ten or fifteen years from now, praise leaders may arise from that very group of children who have long forgotten who first struck the match of their fiery passion. *God hasn't forgotten.*

That's another reason I love church. When it truly reflects the heart of God, no one's job is insignificant. For crying out loud, no one's *life* is insignificant. Our churches are meant to be havens where the caste rules of the world do not apply. A parent might really have to do some searching and praying, but somewhere out there is a gathering of believers so filled with the fruit of the Spirit that an adolescent outcast at school can find love and acceptance at church. If it can't be found, we can all expect Christ to take us to task one day over what we did as His church in our generation. A body of believers can be a life jacket to a soul that otherwise might have drowned in rejection. Oh, I know. There are many exceptions. Churches are no more perfect than the people within them. However, I am ecstatic to tell you that after some measure of fairly extensive research over the last fifteen or so years, I am far from cynical. Those whose hearts God has stolen are the most loving, giving, and forgiving people on the face of the earth. My children need to know them. Your children need to know them . . . so that one day they may be among them.

I've been asked many times, "How do you get your children to go to church?" Well . . . we drive them there in the car. I really do understand what is meant by the question. Getting children to do *anything* they don't want to do is challenging, but some things are too important to decide by popular vote. One of the surest ways that church will become part of our children's lives—*and* that our children's lives will become part of church—is to start as early as possible, seek a church with *life* in it, and take the weekly option out of it. Of course there are exceptions like much-needed family vacations, but approaching church on Sunday just as certainly as school on Monday is the next best thing to a guarantee. Through this approach, attending church becomes part of our lifestyle rather than a hit-or-miss option. Another way to encourage our children's participation is to set the example, not only by church attendance, but by plugging in and getting involved.

I got a huge kick out of the way I heard a brother in Christ answer his children when asked if they *had* to go to church on the following Sunday. He looked at them quite cheerfully and responded, "No, you don't *have* to go to church. You *get* to! Aren't we blessed?" They rolled their eyes way back then, but they're not rolling their eyes anymore.

One of those children is in college now a thousand miles from home. She doesn't have anyone looking over her shoulder to make her attend anymore. But every single Sunday morning, she sets her alarm and heads to a church, no matter how late she was up the night before. Why? Because being part of a church was something her parents presented to her as greatly valuable. A joyful privilege. A happy responsibility entrusted to the people of God. The way she sees it, she *gets to.*

I have no few reasons for being a proponent of church life. Not the least of my reasons would be that when there's trouble at home, a young person may find respite at church. God alone knows the number of young lives through the generations that have stayed afloat during the storms of home by tying their rafts on a regular basis to the docks of church. Oh, thank you, Lord, for shelters in the storm. I am so grateful for my church upbringing. I have as many memories of my childhood at church as I do at home. I was involved up to my ears, but I can't think of a thing I regret doing. I cannot make that claim about another single part of my life. I am utterly convinced with the war brewing in my young soul that if I had not been involved in church, I would have ended up so entirely strung out somewhere I wouldn't have known my way home.

These things kept the echo of God's voice in my troubled ears: I was in children's mission organizations before I could spell *missions.* I was involved in Sunday school—not just in weekly lessons, but in countless opportunities to practice those lessons, such as visiting the lonely in nursing homes and collecting toys for the poor at Christmas. I either attended or served in Vacation Bible School every single summer of my life until I was thirty-seven years old. I was in preschool choir, children's choir, and youth choir. They never could make a singer out of me, but a praiser? Yes, indeed! I was even in the handbell choir. Before you laugh, I loved it! Hands down, it was my all-time favorite! As a matter of fact, I don't think I would ever have taught my first Bible study if I hadn't been rejected by the handbell choir at my church.

When we first joined our (very large and talented) church way back in the early eighties, I prissed myself right into the music office and told them I would love to be considered for the handbell choir. Boy, did they have a fine one! I gave a verbal resume of all the churches where I had played while the woman at the desk looked most unimpressed. She stared at me dryly then said something that I knew to interpret, "Don't call us. We'll call you." *I'm still waiting.* I was devastated. Soon after that, an opening for a Sunday school teacher to real, live women arose. (As opposed to real, small children.) I had never done anything like that in my life. But I took it. After all, I didn't have anything else to do. I laugh every time I think about all the creative ways God gets us where He wants us. When Keith and I have the privilege to see God do something really awesome in the area of women's Bible study, he loves to poke fun at me and ask, "Honey, don't you wish you had stuck with the handbell choir?" The truth be known, I'm still a closet bell ringer. I'd gladly hold my sword with one hand and ring a bell with the other.

As dear as my childhood memories in church are to me, dearer still are those that involve my own children. Amanda was the doll of the church nursery. Melissa was the night-mare. From the time she was only four or five months old, the only way the workers could keep her from screaming was to sit her on the half door of the nursery, hold on to her squirming body as tightly as they could, and let her watch the action in the hall. Those were the good old days. When children turn five, our church invites them into "big church." Translation: they "get to" go to the worship service with their parents. Amanda was perfectly behaved. I haven't heard a sermon since Melissa came into "big church" in 1987.

One of the dearest of all my church memories is the baptism of each of my children. Amanda was six years old when she announced, "Guess what, Mommy! I asked Jesus into my heart!" I was caught totally off guard. "When did you do such a thing?" I asked. I had always pictured how I would be the one to pray with my children to receive Christ. "Last night in my own bed. It was just me and Jesus. Is that not OK?" I pulled my silly self together and said, "Of course it is, sweetheart. Of course it is. Just tell me all about it." I was convinced she understood her decision, but I felt that we should wait until she was a little older to be baptized. I wanted her to remember it forever. I suggested that if she felt the same way when she turned seven, we would progress toward public baptism. Many months passed. The morning of her seventh birthday, I was awakened by her tender little voice whispering in my ear, "He's still in there." It was so precious. She was baptized a short time later.

Keith and I were so proud. *Melissa was furious.* She knew that at our church a person could take the Lord's Supper if she had received Christ and followed His example with believer's baptism. Just before the next ordinance, Melissa announced, "I am asking Jesus into my heart." She was only five. "You are? Honey, that's wonderful! What has brought you to such an important decision?" Her response nearly slew me, but I had to push the hold button on my laughter and save it for later: "Because I'm as hungry as anybody at church." Needless to say, we waited a while.

Melissa grew up considerably over those next two years and decided there was more to receiving Christ than eating in church. She looked like an angel in the baptistry. I was scared to death she'd take the opportunity to address the church body while she had their attention, but, thankfully, she resisted. She did, however, maintain a keen interest in the Lord's Supper, asking me repeatedly when the next occasion would be. She hated for her big sister to get to do *anything* before she did, and she had waited several long years. Finally the weekend arrived.

To my heart's dismay, she developed a stomach virus Saturday night. I finally got her to sleep around 2:00 A.M. A few hours later I crawled out of bed and whispered to Keith, "I need you to stay home with Lissy if you don't mind. She can't possibly go to church, and I've got a class to teach. Is that OK?"

He responded astutely, "Am I going to be the lucky one to tell her she's not going to church to take the Lord's Supper today?"

I retorted, "That's the plan." We both chuckled.

My plan backfired, however, when Melissa caught me sneaking out the door. She looked so sick and her face was dreadfully pale. Still, she yelled, "Mom! You can't leave without me! I'm taking the Lord's Supper today."

My heart just broke. "Baby, you have been sick all night. Not only that, you are terribly contagious. I am so, so sorry, but you can't possibly go today."

She burst into tears. Her next words are etched in my memory forever: "Then can you just get it *to go?*" I suddenly pictured a drive-through window at my church and one of our pastors handing out a white paper bag. I nearly died. She was so sincere that I had to push the hold button again and save it for later.

Needless to say, we didn't get the Lord's Supper *to go.* But I did borrow some little cups from my church, run by the grocery store, and get just the right kind of grape juice and crackers. That afternoon, we had our own little worship service. We sang, read the Scriptures, prayed, then partook of the Lord's table right there in our den. God didn't mind. We felt His presence there in the middle of us. To this day, it is one of the most precious memories of an ordinance that I have stored in this feeble mind of mine.

As special as our home-style worship service was, we didn't make a rule out of observing the ordinances at home. The next Sunday, we were right back in our places, taking part in corporate study and worship. You see, the home was never meant to replace the church any more than the church was meant to replace the home. Even in the "home churches" that congregate around the world, the two influences are distinct. Home and church were meant to complement one another . . . and help one another out. Christ was raised in a home *and* a house of corporate worship. He still has an affinity for showing up at both. When He drops by the church, may He find choir teachers kneeling, children singing, seekers studying, and worshipers worshiping. Some things you just can't get "to go."

Just the two of us.

CHAPTER 18

ONE SLIGHTLY GRAY, WELL-SEASONED MAN

I have had such fun looking under beds and in closets for any feathers my sparrows left behind. Some I've found in unexpected places, like the crumpled Kleenex and the index cards. Others dangle in my memory every single day like the string on the drawer knob. From a green cap and gown I can hold in my hands to a fragrance I can only hold in my heart, each feather has tickled a memory that is precious to me. Priceless. Even when it hurt. My sparrows have sprung from the nest, but the feathers they left behind are mine to keep forever. Nothing can take them from me. Perhaps with the exception of one, the dearest of all.

The one who shaved his beard at my bathroom mirror this morning while I wrapped my hair around large pink Velcro rollers. The one who pledged his life to me well over twenty years ago and meant what he said. Even when I didn't make it easy for him. The one who said in our first year of marriage, "You can get in that car and leave me if you want to. But you'll look in that rearview mirror and there I will be because we are *married* and married is what we're going to stay." While Keith feels that his religious upbringing left his spiritual life lacking in some ways, he had a respect for the institution of marriage that I did not have. *Oh, thank you, Lord, for giving me a man who would not give up.* Of all the wonderful things the children left behind, I am most grateful that I still glance across that nest and see their daddy perched nearby . . . even when he can't see *me* for the newspaper in his hands.

This morning while I was having my quiet time, I found a card someone had tucked in my Bible on Sunday. I could have a garage sale from all the things I have stuck in my Bible, but the Lord intended for me to find and open this little note today . . . before I wrote this reflection. The card came from a dear woman of God whom I've never met face-to-face. She simply mailed it to my church in hopes that I would receive it. *I did.* She spent most of the last year very ill. Seven weeks were spent in the ICU of their local hospital. Her husband attentively cared for her and after many tenuous months, her health was finally restored. A short time later, God called her precious mate of fifty years to his heavenly home. *She told me she misses him.* I sat and cried with her. She wrote me to say that I'd be glad to know God's Word is carrying her through this deep valley. I knew God had further purpose where I was concerned, however. He wanted to remind me before I wrote this final reflection that the most precious things in this earthly life are those we cannot hold in our grasp forever.

Part of a caring marriage is learning to love one another through *reasonable idiosyncrasies.* My expression may sound like an oxymoron, but I don't think it is. Let's face it. Some of our idiosyncrasies or peculiarities arise from a pure lack of emotional health, and we don't need to expect *others* to deal with them. *We* need to deal with them and let God heal us from them. On the other hand, some are more reasonable. Like *mine,* for instance. I'm only teasing, but there's an element of truth in the attitude, isn't there? Our own are "understandable." Everyone else's are white-coat certifiable, right?

I had to come to a place where I realized that not all of my peculiarities and preferences were reasonable, and those were the ones I needed to lose. But a few aren't too terribly imposing, and I've hung on to them pretty tightly in the name of individuality. For instance, I love to eat chili, but something about rinsing out the pan afterward is distasteful to me. I know it's silly and I'm sure Keith does, too, but after all these years, if I'll cook it, he'll cheerfully clean it up.

One of Keith's little quirks is that he likes for us to leave for work at the same time in the morning. He suffered so many primary losses in his young life. *His older brother. His younger sister.* So many people he was closest to left him behind. And *alone.* He's dealt with those losses, but they dealt him a few understandable preferences. We don't make a big deal out of it. We don't delve into the deep psychological dimensions of it. I just know he prefers we leave at the same time. So on most mornings, our neighbors will see one of us pull out of the driveway right after the other. The card in my Bible reminded me that the day will probably come when we don't leave together. When one of us will leave the other behind. My heart broke at the thought. So many years. So much life. So many things shared with no one else. He's my very best friend. I can't even imagine one of us without the other. We've even fought over who needs the other most. Keith isn't even ashamed to admit he hopes he pulls out of the "driveway" first. But if he does, I told him I'd run over him.

Life is full of so many paradoxes. Like how most spouses lose one another when they can no longer remember life without the other. When their lives have been thrown in the domestic blender for so long, they don't have a clue where one starts and the other ends. *Kind of like mixed fruit.* Like that precious woman who sent me the card. She and her husband had fifty years together! Fifty times they gathered around the Thanksgiving table, giving gratitude to God whether they'd had little or much that year. Fifty Christmas mornings they awoke to one another, whether an infant was in the nursery, a student was home from college, or the house otherwise echoed with emptiness. *They had each other.* Fifty times they were there to celebrate the other's birthday. From the early days when they blew out the candles to the latter days when they were too afraid they'd blow out their dentures. They went from pimples to wrinkles with one another. Bicycles to bifocals. Good times. Bad times. Pretty times. And pretty ugly times. *They were partners.* They swept each other off their feet when they were young, and they helped each other to their feet when they were old. They held each other's hands for fifty years. Then the grasp of one grew faint. Then cold.

No, I'm not at all sure how a leftover soul stands that. Only through the grace of God granted according to our need.

Still. No matter how much harder it might be to let go, I hope Keith and I have the balance of fifty years with one another. After all, that was the term of our "lease," you may recall. He and I may be a mighty long way from the day we no longer pull out of the driveway together, but this I know for sure: I can imagine life without Keith far less now than I could have ten years ago. For couples that are willing, marriage gets richer and the dividing lines grayer. He and I say something to one another often: "I love *old* love. It's so much better than *new* love." *That it is.* We may have heartburn more often than heart flutters these days, but I wouldn't trade in what we have *now* for all we had *way back when* for anything. I love old love. Maybe I have a million reasons, but if you'll permit me a final family indulgence, I believe I'll share a few.

I love how I know the exact expression on his face the moment he answers the phone. I love the hair-thin scar on his hand and how no matter how much older his hand looks, it's still there. I love how he's the only person on the face of the earth that loves my children like I do. I love how I often know exactly what he's going to say when I tell him something. Then I love how he shocks me by saying something that reminds me he's still got a lot of mystery in him. I love how he never runs out of big words that I have to look up. *And I'm not always happy I did.* I love how he stops off at any kids or pets that happen to be between the front door and me to offer some affection when he comes in after work. Then he always says, "I've gotta get to your mama." I wait and grin. I love how the girls have always known they were his princesses but no one has ever doubted who was his *queen.* Ah, yes. That's how it should be.

I love looking as forward to his hunting and fishing magazines coming in the mail as he does because I like to be the one to give them to him. I love how we can practically read each other's minds on occasions and can nearly die laughing without a single word being said. I love the gray in his beard. I love how safe I feel when he's home. I love trying to look on the good side of his snoring: at least I know he's still alive. I love knowing which is his "good" ear and which is his "bad" ear. I love double-checking to make sure he has his earplugs when he goes to shoot skeet. I love how he always said, "Now, girls, we're gonna have to clean up all this mess. You know how your mama hates this." I do! I love how he knew me so well that he got us *another* new puppy even after I told him I'd have a fit. I love how *I* knew he'd never make the puppy sleep outside even though he promised me he would. I love how he said just last night, "Hop up in the bed with your mama, Beenie. You know she can't sleep a wink without a good bird dog snuggled up next to her." And I laughed. I love how we can be in a group of people, but I can look across at one person in the whole room and say, "He is mine." *And I am his.* I love knowing that Keith cannot stand the thought of ever living without me. Nor I him. I love knowing that when we have to, it will only be for a little while. And that God knows best who should pull out of the driveway first. I love that for both of us, the driveway of earth leads straight to the driveway of heaven. I love being more anxious to see what God has stored up for Keith than what he has stored up for me. (I hope he gets a hot rod. I just want a bird dog.)

And maybe best of all the earthly things, I love how we still haven't changed each other nearly as much as we swore we would. And we're glad we didn't. Keith got me a fishing pole on our first Valentine's Day together. He took me to the lake and gave me only one instruction: "Just don't wrap the line around that tree right there." The lure has been dangling from that branch ever since. I didn't mean to. Honestly, it was the only place I tried *not* to cast. Thankfully, he didn't give *me* up . . . but he gave up trying to make a fisherman out of me. I never became a hunter either. But I do dearly love going to the cabin at the deer lease, building a fire, roasting marshmallows, drinking hot chocolate, and surveying the critters. Keith has done the same for me. No, he didn't become a cookie cutter of everything I thought I wanted—and I have no doubt I'm the better for it. What a brat I would've been . . . if I could've been. Thus far, he hasn't surrendered his life to the ministry—*except for mine*—nor has he accepted a nomination for deacon, but I wouldn't trade him for a handpick of all the preachers in Texas. Goodness knows the man has been as patient with all my likes and dislikes as I ever thought about being with his. A man who has always been more prone to shoot a bird than watch one, he puts up with all my bird talk, birdhouses, bird feeders, and birdbaths. He buys me bird books and will take me almost anywhere to bird-watch while staring at me completely, lovingly . . . *mystified.* Some years ago, while we were vacationing in Colorado and the kids were making their usual sport of me, he said dryly, "You may as well quit making fun of your mother. We're going to find her a Western Mountain Bluebird if it's the last thing we do." *And it was.* Just before we pulled out of the state park, one landed on the gate. We all screamed and clapped, and it flew away in the nick of time. Had Keith had a BB gun, he might have offered to shoot it, stuff it, and let me keep it for a souvenir. We appear destined to stay Beth the librarian and Keith the barbarian.

We are a planet away from understanding one another completely. Sometimes we just stare at one another in total wonder. Wondering, *What kind of alien are you?* Ah, that's part of the beauty of it. You see, spouses who claim the other got boring just quit getting to know them. To share an uncommon love where we have uncommon ground—now, *that's* marriage.

Nah. We don't have a perfect one. But we have a good one. And for now, a happy one . . . which is nothing less than a miracle. That's why we wrote this book. Yes, *we.* This one is from all of us. Keith, Amanda, Melissa, and me. One of us penned it, but we all lived it and agreed that we, an otherwise fairly private family, would extend it as a testimony to the grace of God. We would have just shared our own stories around the dinner table over take-out food if we didn't feel like we had something to say that another family might need to hear. *We are a miracle.* Every strike was against us. Keith and I had enough baggage to sink the *Titanic.* The kids could have inherited enough generational junk to keep them and their children in bondage every day of their lives. But here we are. Crazier about each other than we are crazy. Oh, if you only knew how amazing that is!

We're making it. And so can you. Only one thing stood between us and a scattered nest. *God.* Ever loving us, forgiving us, teaching us, restoring us. Redeeming our failures. Reclaiming our surrendered ground. Repairing our broken wings. As Psalm 91:4 says, He covered us with His feathers. And they are all over our nest.